CHRIS BUSH

Chris Bush is a Sheffield-born playwright, lyricist and theatremaker. Past work includes *The Last Noël* (Old Fire Station/Attic Theatre); *Pericles* (Olivier, National Theatre); *A Declaration from the People* (Dorfman, National Theatre); *The Changing Room* (National Theatre Connections Festival); *The Assassination of Katie Hopkins* (Theatr Clwyd); *Standing at the Sky's Edge*, *Steel*, *What We Wished For*, *A Dream*, *The Sheffield Mysteries*, *20 Tiny Plays about Sheffield* (Sheffield Theatres); *Scenes from the End of the World* (CSSD: Yard Theatre); *Transcending* (Orange Tree Theatre); *Larksong* (New Vic Theatre); *Cards on the Table* (Royal Exchange Theatre); *ODD* (Royal & Derngate, Northampton: concert performance); *Sleight & Hand* (Summerhall/Odeon Cinemas/BBC Arts); *TONY! The Blair Musical* (York Theatre Royal/tour); *Speaking Freely*, *Poking the Bear* (Theatre503); *The Bureau of Lost Things* (Theatre503/Rose Bruford); *Wolf* (Latitude Festival). Chris has won the National Young Playwrights' Festival, a Brit Writers' Award and the Perfect Pitch Award. She has previously been Playwright in Residence for Sheffield Theatres, and part of writers' groups at the National Theatre, Orange Tree and Royal Exchange, Manchester.

T0346857

Other Titles in this Series

Chris Bush

FAUSTUS: THAT DAMNED WOMAN

NICK HERN BOOKS

London

www.nickhernbooks.co.uk

A Nick Hern Book

Faustus: That Damned Woman first published in Great Britain as a paperback original in 2020 by Nick Hern Books Limited, The Glasshouse, 49a Goldhawk Road, London W12 8QP

Faustus: That Damned Woman copyright © 2020 Chris Bush

Chris Bush has asserted her right to be identified as the author of this work

Cover photograph of Jodie McNee by Helen Maybanks

Designed and typeset by Nick Hern Books, London
Printed in Great Britain by Mimeo Ltd, Huntingdon, Cambridgeshire PE29 6XX

A CIP catalogue record for this book is available from the British Library

ISBN 978 1 84842 931 4

Woodland
CARBON
www.woodlandcarbon.co.uk
NICK HERN BOOKS
Printed on Carbon Captured paper

Introduction
Chris Bush

The Faust myth is one of the great stories of the Western canon – a man (because it is almost always a man) strikes a deal for greatness and pays a terrible price for it. The original Johann Georg Faust was a fifteenth-century German alchemist, astronomer and magician, whose rumoured exploits inspired the works of Marlowe, Goethe, Berlioz and others, but the idea of a diabolical pact with undesirable consequences goes back much further, and exists in thousands of different forms.

It is, in essence, a morality tale. It teaches us to be careful of what we wish for, that pride comes before a fall, that nothing comes for free. Faustus is bored by the limits of his mortality (and his humanity) and so seeks supernatural aid. Only when the Devil comes to claim his due does Faustus finally realise he has reached too far. He begs forgiveness, but it's too late – he's made his bed and now he must lie in it.

The story endures because greed endures, and ambition endures, and we are never short of contemporary figures who believe they can beat the system, or that the rules needn't apply to them. A modern Faustus might be a tech billionaire, a doctor playing God, or an unscrupulous politician signing over his soul to a Mephistophelian fixer – the only part that may feel like a stretch is that in most versions, Faustus gets his comeuppance.

In the UK, we're perhaps most familiar with Marlowe's *Doctor Faustus,* which for all its genius can also be deeply unsatisfying. The text thoroughly derails itself in the middle, primarily because Faustus doesn't really do anything of note with his powers. He is granted near unlimited gifts and he squanders them pulling pranks and playing tricks. This is partially because Marlowe's Faustus never has a real need for the Devil. He is already a successful medical doctor whose 'bills [are] hung up as monuments, whereby whole cities have escaped the plague'. He's on top as it is. Now, the story of a man who has everything and yet still yearns for more is not uninteresting, but it feels like a missed opportunity.

My Faustus is a young woman in seventeenth-century London with no wealth and little agency, living on the fringes of society. When she comes to meet Lucifer she understands what's at stake, but sees his offer as the least-worst option available to her. She sells her soul not out of greed or boredom, but in order to control her own destiny. Of course this is only the beginning of the story, and despite the Devil's assistance, Faustus continues to be treated differently because of her sex (and social class). Through this, *That Damned Woman* becomes a study of how we judge women who pursue greatness, and how traits that seem admirable in men here might warrant literal damnation.

The regendering of figures from classical literature isn't a fad or a fashion. As I see it, the purpose is twofold. Firstly, it's one useful, practical way we can redress the gender imbalance that still exists across our stages. The Western canon is dominated by male leads, and our industry is stuffed with incredible women who shouldn't be relegated to always playing someone's wife or someone's mother. Secondly, and perhaps more significantly, it makes the work more interesting. Inserting a woman into a traditionally male narrative complicates things. It creates more edges and obstacles. It highlights the way in which women still operate in a world designed by and for men, and their very presence can send a story we think we know into strange and exciting directions.

The Faust myth is robust, and endures because it is universal. This is still the same story of vaulting ambition, hubris and exceptionalism, of what we're prepared to sacrifice to achieve greatness, of the tantalising thought that despite all the evidence, we might finally be the one to outsmart the devil. None of this is lost by having a female Faustus, and she is still just as vainglorious and headstrong and morally compromised as any other iteration. She just happens to be a woman, and that means her narrative plays out in a different way. We should always be striving to fill our stages with women just as messy, complicated and conflicted as any of their male counterparts.

Faustus: That Damned Woman was commissioned by Headlong and Lyric Hammersmith Theatre as part of an ongoing commitment to commissioning new works of scale from women writers. It was first performed at the Lyric Hammersmith Theatre, London, on 28 January 2020 (previews from 22 January), in a co-production between Headlong and Lyric Hammersmith Theatre, in association with Birmingham Repertory Theatre. The cast was as follows:

CORNELIA/JENNY/ALICE	Katherine Carlton
VIOLET/MARIE	Alicia Charles
KATHERINE/DOCTOR GARRETT/ISABEL	Emmanuella Cole
JOHANNA FAUSTUS	Jodie McNee
THOMAS/LUCIFER	Barnaby Power
NEWBURY/JUDGE/PIERRE	Tim Samuels
MEPHISTOPHELES	Danny Lee Wynter

Director	Caroline Byrne
Set Designer	Ana Inés Jabares-Pita
Costume Designer	Line Bech
Lighting Designer	Richard Howell
Composer and Sound Designer	Giles Thomas
Video Designer	Ian William Galloway
Movement Director	Shelley Maxwell
Casting Director	Annelie Powell CDG
Associate Director	Ebenezer Bamgboye
Costume Supervisor	Jackie Orton
Fight Director	Rachel Bown-Williams of Rc-Annie Ltd
Associate Fight Director	Bethan Clark of Rc-Annie Ltd
Voice Coach	Tess Dignan
Intimacy Co-Ordinator	Jess Tucker Boyd
Casting Associate	Hayley Kaimakliotis CDG
Production Manager	Tom Lee
Company Stage Manager	Paul C Deavin
Deputy Stage Manager	Alex Burke
Assistant Stage Manager	Kirsten Buckmaster
Head of Wardrobe/ Assistant Costume Supervisor	Vicki Halliday
Head of Video	David Brown
Wardrobe Assistant	Velia Ansorg

For Roni, my damned woman

Characters

1600s
KATHERINE, *Johanna's mother*
WITCHFINDER
JUDGE

JOHANNA FAUSTUS

VIOLET
CORNELIA, *her daughter*

THOMAS, *Johanna's father*

DOCTOR NEWBURY

MEPHISTOPHELES
LUCIFER

ISABEL, *Newbury's wife*

1800s–1900s
SINGER
ELIZABETH GARRETT
MARIE CURIE
PIERRE CURIE

2000s onwards
VIDEO VOICE-OVER
JENNY

WAR
FAMINE
PESTILENCE

ALICE

Doubling all negotiable. Other non-speaking parts played by the company.

This text went to press before the end of rehearsals and so may differ slightly from the play as performed.

ACT ONE

Scene One

Essex, 1645/London 1665.

In London, JOHANNA FAUSTUS, VIOLET *and* CORNELIA *gather. A ceremony of sorts is taking place – rustic, earthy, no airs and graces. In front of them is a large, wide bucket/basin of water.* CORNELIA *is nervous.* VIOLET *looks to* FAUSTUS. FAUSTUS *nods, and* VIOLET *and* CORNELIA *thrust* FAUSTUS*'s head down into the water. On this, we snap to –*

1645. Essex. A cell. KATHERINE *appears, soaking wet and shivering, having just been dunked as part of her witch trial. She has survived, just. She gasps for air. The* WITCHFINDER *is with her, as is a silent* GUARD.

WITCHFINDER. There you have it.

KATHERINE. Please –

WITCHFINDER. See how she could not be drowned? That is the Devil's doing.

KATHERINE. No.

WITCHFINDER. How else could she survive it?

KATHERINE. I'm not… Always swam, ever since a girl. Always strong.

WITCHFINDER. Supernatural strong.

KATHERINE. No. I promise. I promise.

WITCHFINDER. Unnatural murderer.

KATHERINE. Babies die sometimes – I never –

WITCHFINDER. If doubt remains, put her back under.

In 1665, FAUSTUS *comes up from the water, spluttering. Lights down on 1645.*

FAUSTUS. Did you see her? Again.

> VIOLET *and* CORNELIA *thrust her head back under again. Snap back to –*

> *1645.* KATHERINE *is being walked round in a circle by the* WITCHFINDER. *She is beyond exhaustion. She stumbles.*

WITCHFINDER. Keep her moving. Don't let her stop.

KATHERINE. Can't.

WITCHFINDER. On your feet.

KATHERINE. No.

WITCHFINDER. Then confess.

KATHERINE. Need my daughter.

WITCHFINDER. It ends when you confess.

> *Suddenly,* KATHERINE *pounces on the* WITCHFINDER, *knocking him to the floor.*

KATHERINE. Little man, little man, little man. The Devil will come for you too.

> The GUARD *hauls her off as we snap back into 1665,* FAUSTUS *hauled out of the water, coughing spluttering.*

VIOLET. Steady.

FAUSTUS. Keep going. I can keep going.

> FAUSTUS *goes back under. Back to 1645.* KATHERINE*'s mouth is gagged, hands bound.*

WITCHFINDER. You have seen how Lucifer speaks through her, gives her unnatural strength, provokes in her these outbursts –

> KATHERINE *lunges toward him.*

And now we shall uncover where he left his mark on her. (*To the* GUARD.) Take off her dress.

> KATHERINE *struggles. Back into 1665.* FAUSTUS *brought out of the water again.*

FAUSTUS. More.

VIOLET. That's enough now.

FAUSTUS. No. I'm close. Please.

More reluctantly, VIOLET *and* CORNELIA *put her head back under. Into –*

1645. KATHERINE *is at the scaffold, gagged, a rope around her neck. A* JUDGE *intones.*

JUDGE. Katherine Faustus, you have been found guilty of witchcraft, of conspiring with the Devil and signing your name in his book, of laying curses upon Goody Francis, and of the brewing of poisons resulting in the death of Owen Francis, not yet three months old. Therefore you are sentenced to be hanged by the neck until dead, and may God have mercy on your immortal soul. Do you have anything to say?

KATHERINE*'s gag is removed.*

KATHERINE. Johanna? Where is she? Is she – ?

JUDGE. Calm yourself.

KATHERINE. Should bring her, should see. If she doesn't see she'll only imagine it, and that'll be worse. Could anything be worse? Where is she?

JUDGE. This is your last opportunity to repent. Confess your sins and name your conspirators –

KATHERINE. And ask forgiveness?

JUDGE. Yes. And our Lord Jesus Christ in His Almighty –

KATHERINE. Forgive me then. Forgive me, Johanna. Forgive me, precious child. Wicked mother you have. They shall call me wicked and I can't deny it. Most monstrous of all, to leave you here. I am abandoning you in the forest when you are a seedling still. Unnatural. Abhorrent, not to see you grown. Could I not have a little more time? One minute more. One minute and I could stretch each second to last a lifetime. Where is she?

JUDGE. Address your saviour.

KATHERINE. Saviour, yes. Saved by her – I will be. I had so much more to teach you. Names of plants and trees and the spaces in between things where the old words fail us and we have to invent our own. So much invention –

JUDGE. That's enough.

KATHERINE. Never enough.

JUDGE. If you have nothing to say to the Lord –

KATHERINE. Not to him. Not to you. Damn you both. But to her –

JUDGE. Very well.

KATHERINE. The Devil take you.

The rope tightens. KATHERINE *spreads her arms out and for a second almost appears to fly. Then suddenly any calm/confidence disappears. She reaches forward.*

Wait!

A sense of a rope jerking upwards before the image disappears into darkness.

Scene Two

London, 1665.

Immediately following on, CORNELIA *and* VIOLET *haul* FAUSTUS *out of the water. For a moment she seems limp, unresponsive.*

VIOLET. Johanna? Come on, girl.

VIOLET *coaxes some of the water out of* FAUSTUS *and she splutters back to life.*

Easy now.

FAUSTUS. Was that real? Is she real?

VIOLET. Yes.

FAUSTUS. Not a trick?

CORNELIA. No.

FAUSTUS. So where is she now? She must be *somewhere* – somewhere in the space between things.

CORNELIA. With you. Within you.

FAUSTUS. No. No, I know that much. She's not been with me for twenty years. I should've tried to find her sooner.

VIOLET. We should all be going – before we're missed.

FAUSTUS. Does the Devil have her?

VIOLET. We don't deal with the Devil.

FAUSTUS. But did she? (*Beat.*) What they said about her, was that…? She saw things sometimes too – things in people they didn't even know about themselves. And she was – she was strong.

VIOLET. Nothing strange about strength.

FAUSTUS. And I remember she used to tell me – she said if I misbehaved, the crows in the field would come and tell her. But that's not… Is that just the sort of thing that mothers say?

VIOLET. Most likely.

FAUSTUS. Will you ask her? Please? You brought me out too soon.

VIOLET. You almost drowned. Leave her in peace now.

FAUSTUS. What peace? No. You heard her. She went unfinished. She had more to say. (*To* CORNELIA.) Take me back under.

CORNELIA. I can't.

FAUSTUS. I'm strong – strong like she was – I can take it.

CORNELIA. Not tonight.

FAUSTUS. Please. Once more. Hold me down. I'm not afraid.

VIOLET. It isn't safe.

FAUSTUS. What are you afraid of?

VIOLET. Forces far beyond you.

FAUSTUS. I can pay you more. Not now – not right now, but
I promise –

CORNELIA. I'm sorry.

VIOLET. Maybe at the next full moon. (*To* CORNELIA.) Come
now.

FAUSTUS. So that's it? And I shall see you knelt at St Mary's
on Sunday, should you dare – should you not catch fire
crossing the threshold. I sought you out because I thought
you could *do* something.

VIOLET. Try to sleep.

FAUSTUS. I don't sleep! (*Beat.*) There was a preacher I heard
down Bankside talking about the End Days – God
abandoning us – and I thought 'Only now?' I saw a woman
laid out in the street, boils all over, her shroud had blown
away, and she looked so like her – like my mother – in so
much pain. And what if that was eternal? Strung up here then
damned forever after. I have to know.

VIOLET. Another night.

FAUSTUS. Cornelia? Please. You saw her too – summoned her.
Let me take your hand, just for a second. Let me be close
to her.

She holds out her hand. As CORNELIA *reaches for it,*
FAUSTUS *grabs her arm and twists it up behind her back.*
CORNELIA *yelps with pain.*

VIOLET. Let go of her!

FAUSTUS. Oh, Cornelia, what a curse it is to be the witch's
daughter.

CORNELIA. Please –

FAUSTUS. What was she? My mother – what was she?

CORNELIA. You're hurting me.

FAUSTUS. Was she wicked? Is she damned?

CORNELIA. I don't know!

FAUSTUS. Then you must ask her.

> FAUSTUS *pushes* CORNELIA *to her knees, and is now trying to force her head into the basin of water.* VIOLET *gets involved, and eventually succeeds in hauling her off and pulling* CORNELIA *away.*

VIOLET. Enough now! Look at you. You aren't special, Johanna Faustus, nor was your mother, I'd wager – just as mad as you are.

FAUSTUS. Don't say that. Don't call me that.

VIOLET. Pray you we don't cross paths again.

FAUSTUS. But does the Devil have her?

VIOLET. You'd have to ask him yourself.

> VIOLET *and* CORNELIA *go. Straight into –*

Scene Three

London, 1665.

We are now in the house of FAUSTUS *and her father.* FAUSTUS *is knelt on the floor collecting herself. She feels a presence behind her.*

A tall figure dressed in a long, waxed coat appears. A beaked plague mask and wide hat or hood obscures their face. A sinister image.

When FAUSTUS *turns to the figure she isn't surprised or afraid. The figure removes their mask. This is* THOMAS, *her father, a plague doctor. The spell is broken.*

FAUSTUS. Good day, Father.

THOMAS. Little good in it.

THOMAS *begins to take off his boots and cloak for* FAUSTUS *to put away.*

FAUSTUS. Who have you seen?

THOMAS. The Cartwrights have lost two more. Just leaves Mary now.

FAUSTUS. Mary? She's stronger than I thought.

THOMAS. Not yet nine, and now without a soul to take her in.

FAUSTUS. She's no one left? (*Beat.*) And another family who shall never pay us, I suppose.

THOMAS. Johanna –

FAUSTUS. We must eat too.

THOMAS. We're not short of custom. I swear I passed three fresh-dug pits this morning. (*Beat.*) She said she had an aunt in Canterbury – Mary – would come to fetch her. We might make her up a bed, until then.

FAUSTUS. Here?

THOMAS. There's room enough.

FAUSTUS. But she is –

THOMAS. What is our mission? What is the motto hanging above our door? Recite.

FAUSTUS (*with some reluctance*). '*Opiferque Per Orbem Dicor.*'

THOMAS. Translated?

FAUSTUS. 'And throughout the world I am called the bringer of help.'

THOMAS. And what is our duty?

FAUSTUS. To save as many as we can, but –

THOMAS. No buts.

FAUSTUS. The aunt shall never come. It takes a saint or a madman to enter London now.

THOMAS (*snapping*). Or just a decent soul, Johanna, unlike your own! (*Sighs.*) Are those my poultices?

FAUSTUS. Yes.

THOMAS. Finished?

FAUSTUS. Almost.

FAUSTUS *will see to this task as the scene continues.*

THOMAS. Lazy. Insolent. And these traits I do my best to correct, but to be so uncaring –

FAUSTUS. I do care. If you get sick –

THOMAS. Then the Lord wills it, but we still do his work.

FAUSTUS (*giving up*). The mint is past its best, but there's dried lavender and camomile. No orange either. We still have some clove.

THOMAS. And more leeches for me?

FAUSTUS. Dandelion too. Elderflower, nettle and willow bark. No one else touches it – no one knows what they're looking for in the city. They do better in a tea than a balm, if the water's fresh, and there's oats to make a paste from.

THOMAS. The leeches?

FAUSTUS. I didn't get to the ponds today.

THOMAS. They are what I need the most. To watch a creature grow thick and black with blood, drawing the sickness from them – that is medicine – that is science they can see.

FAUSTUS. It does nothing. But these herbs –

THOMAS. No one cares for hedgerow cures here.

FAUSTUS. They can do more than sweeten the air. These bring the fever down – you've seen it.

THOMAS. You shall brew no potions in this house, do you hear me? And pick no weeds where any soul can see you.

FAUSTUS. Mother knew –

THOMAS. And I shall not lose you to it, as I lost her. Your mother was troubled. She had no learning. She was not the apothecary –

FAUSTUS. Then you could teach me.

THOMAS. All that stays in the country where we left it. Stop spending your days in idleness, picking flowers. Learn obedience, follow instruction – I grow tired of trying to improve you, when coaxing you toward any virtue seems to strain against your very nature.

FAUSTUS. Don't say that.

THOMAS. What shall you do, hmm, when I am no longer here to take care of you?

FAUSTUS. I can look after myself.

THOMAS. I fear for you, Johanna.

FAUSTUS. You needn't.

THOMAS. With no one to keep you honest... Edward Allen – now there is a good man.

FAUSTUS. Don't.

THOMAS. An honest man. An upstanding sort of... Almost a year now, since his wife passed.

FAUSTUS. Please.

THOMAS. And I know, I know we both thought you might've missed your chance at that, but as he has a son already –

FAUSTUS. I don't want a son.

THOMAS. He might take you.

FAUSTUS. I don't want him.

THOMAS. Might have the wit to learn this trade. Someone I could safely –

FAUSTUS (*gesturing to the poultices*). These are finished now, as you like them.

THOMAS (*ignoring this*). You must have someone – someone
to keep you tethered, once I'm gone. Promise me –

FAUSTUS. And I'll go to the ponds first thing tomorrow.

THOMAS. I'll write to him – have you deliver... We can make
the offer an attractive one. But you must try –

FAUSTUS. Edward Allen is sick.

THOMAS. What's that?

FAUSTUS. Not long for this world, I heard.

THOMAS. Nonsense. I saw him not a fortnight ago.

FAUSTUS. I had it from his sister on Sunday. Doesn't think
he'll survive it.

THOMAS. Well. Well, if that is... If that proves to be...

FAUSTUS. You'd have me share his sickbed?

THOMAS. I will still find you someone. There must be
someone for you.

   Scene ends. FAUSTUS *steps straight into –*

Scene Four

London, 1665.

FAUSTUS. Well, Faustus, now you know who you must seek.
   My mind is clear, and I am not afraid.
   To summon spirits I was not afraid
   To call the Devil? No, still not afraid,
   If he comes next. I've surely prayed to worse.
   'Twas in the name of our Lord Jesus Christ
   They bound my mother's wrists with sacraments
   Weighted her pockets with their holy books
   And with the word of God they wrung her neck.
   And was that not a very Christian thing?

And was that not a lawful, righteous act?
And was it not the Devil took the blame?
I'll ask him then – I'll put it to him straight –
'They tell me that my mother called on you,
And I cannot believe she'd stoop so low,
But if she did, you did not serve her well.'
And if she did, then is she with you still?
And if she did – though surely she could not –
I'd argue that the Devil's in my debt,
For then she died with naught to show for it.
I say you are a coward, Lucifer,
Who flees the scene and lets the world go hang.
You don't scare me. I swear I'll seek you out.
For I'd sooner be damned than have this doubt.

Into –

Scene Five

London, 1665.

The study of an expensive home. DOCTOR NEWBURY *is before* FAUSTUS.

NEWBURY. I don't normally see people off the street, especially with the streets being what they are. But you said the Earl of Southampton sent you?

FAUSTUS. I did.

NEWBURY. I'd heard he was unwell. What ails him now?

FAUSTUS. I couldn't say.

NEWBURY. What symptoms does he show?

FAUSTUS. I don't know.

NEWBURY. What has he said?

FAUSTUS. Nothing to me. I do not serve the Earl of Southampton, sir. But I did need to speak with you.

NEWBURY (*with a chuckle*). I see.

FAUSTUS. I had to –

NEWBURY. Bold of you.

FAUSTUS. I needed –

NEWBURY. Resourceful, if dishonest. Reckless. (*Beat.*) So what is it – plague?

FAUSTUS. No.

NEWBURY. What marks do you have?

FAUSTUS. I'm not here for that.

NEWBURY. Show me.

FAUSTUS. I'm healthy. I am – my father is an apothecary – I know the signs.

NEWBURY. Then what?

FAUSTUS. You take in women sometimes. Young women, especially – girls, really.

NEWBURY. It has been known.

FAUSTUS. Of few years and little worth. Who won't be missed – not by anyone who matters.

NEWBURY. You want my shelter?

FAUSTUS. I'm looking for someone.

NEWBURY. Ah. A friend?

FAUSTUS. A stranger for now, but I've been looking a while. People look at you like you're mad, when you ask them if they know the Devil. Most people. Or they think you're being poetic. I've no time for poetry.

NEWBURY (*now curious*). You seek the Devil, miss?

FAUSTUS. But they don't look at me like that.

NEWBURY. And why might that be?

FAUSTUS. To ask him a question. (*Beat.*) See round me, people don't invite him into their houses. A bit of witchery, perhaps, a country charm or two, but not him. Not because they're too holy, just afraid. So where does the Devil reside in London? Not round the plague pits like you'd think. Not in Whitechapel. Nice houses like this.

NEWBURY. I don't know what you think you've heard –

FAUSTUS. People whisper, doctor. Messengers, tradesmen, serving girls all whisper. And mothers – good mothers won't let their daughters work here any more. Not once word spread.

NEWBURY. Of what?

FAUSTUS. He cuts them. Bleeds them. Marks them. Worse still, so long as they're virgins. Takes them to his cellar with his acolytes where they drink blood and sing songs and perform strange –

NEWBURY. Enough!

FAUSTUS. All because Doctor Newbury courts the Devil. Desperate to meet him.

NEWBURY (*still presenting good humour*). The stories some women tell.

FAUSTUS. So they lied?

NEWBURY. You believed them? And yet you'd walk so willingly into the lion's den?

FAUSTUS. I am no Daniel, sir, but I would befriend the beast.

A pause. NEWBURY *considers* FAUSTUS *for a moment.*

NEWBURY. You know what those women are used for?

FAUSTUS. I've seen their scars.

NEWBURY. And you would submit to it willingly?

FAUSTUS. I would be an apprentice, not a sacrifice.

NEWBURY. But still you must submit. First to me, in readiness to submit to him, when he comes.

FAUSTUS. If he comes. You've not found him yet, have you? Let me help.

Pause. They regard each other.

NEWBURY. What's your name?

FAUSTUS. Faustus.

NEWBURY. Your first name?

FAUSTUS. Johanna.

NEWBURY. Johanna. You shall call me 'doctor'. You shall not make the mistake of thinking us equal.

FAUSTUS. I do not think that, sir.

NEWBURY. You shall know your place.

FAUSTUS. Yes, doctor, I intend to take it.

NEWBURY (*smiles*). Undress for me. (*Beat.*) There is a plague in this city and I must examine you for signs of it. Take off your clothes.

Into –

Scene Six

London, 1665.

FAUSTUS *is transformed before us. She is exhausted, bloodied, bruised, suffering. She has been pushed to her limits. This change symbolises the months spent under* NEWBURY*'s 'tutelage', though needn't feel like a literal depiction of it.*

A scream is heard. CORNELIA *emerges in a nightshirt. She is joined by* VIOLET.

VIOLET. What is it?

CORNELIA. I saw her.

VIOLET. A bad dream, is all.

CORNELIA. No.

VIOLET. And you're getting too old for nightmares now.

CORNELIA. You know it isn't.

VIOLET. You are to forget all about Johanna Faustus, do you hear?

CORNELIA. But –

VIOLET. Never knew her – never met her.

CORNELIA. You know what she's doing?

VIOLET. None of our concern.

CORNELIA. You've seen what she'll do?

VIOLET. Go back to bed.

CORNELIA. She won't stop until she finds him. Won't stop even then. I've seen it.

VIOLET. You'll wake your father. You don't want –

CORNELIA. Won't stop until the whole world burns beneath her.

VIOLET. Enough now. It was only a dream. We'll hear no more of it.

They go. Into –

Scene Seven

London, 1665.

FAUSTUS *is now on a heath outside London at noon. She carries a bag with her containing various stones/artefacts which she'll use to mark out a circle on the floor, a knife, a scrap of parchment, and torches which she'll light.*

FAUSTUS. Here, Faustus, surely you must have it now?
    Four moons you've toiled in cursed apprenticeship,
    Now use all you have learnt at dire cost,
    Draw on that darkness thick within your veins

And with that fury flush the Devil out.
(*From the parchment.*) *Diabolus… Execrabilis… Satanas…*
Beelzebub inferni ardentis monarcha!
Was all this done to steal Latin scraps?
A fool to think '*Satanas*' speaks this way –
Why, was he born in Rome? No, this is just
The language of the learnèd and corrupt –
Satanas won't trade words with common folk.
But I'll address you plain. Well then, old man,
I think I've figured how to coax you out.
See, Lucifer, you are the Morning Star,
Light-bringer, so they call you – Shining One –
But they only dare face you in the dark.
Not me. I'd meet you when the sun is high,
Out here upon the heath I'll set a fire
And in this faerie circle call your name.
You don't scare me. There's magic here enough.
What else? Must you be lured like leeches then?
You want your taste of flesh?

*She holds out her arm, takes out a knife and cuts into it,
wincing, letting a few drops of blood fall on the ground
inside the circle she's marked out.*

Come out come out wherever you are!
That's all the incantation you'll get.
Come on out if you're coming.

A wind, a rattling.

Here, fishy-fishy-fish.

*The fire blazes blindingly bright for a second and then goes
out.* FAUSTUS *gasps. When we can see her again, her arm
is drenched in blood.* MEPHISTOPHELES *stands inside the
circle, wiping blood from his mouth.*

MEPHISTOPHELES. Madam.

FAUSTUS. I knew you'd bite. So you are Lucifer?

MEPHISTOPHELES. No, ma'am.

FAUSTUS. No?

MEPHISTOPHELES. One who serves him.

FAUSTUS (*sighs*). Another serving boy!

MEPHISTOPHELES. And heard your caterwauling as I passed.

FAUSTUS. I'll have no more intermediaries. Fetch him.

MEPHISTOPHELES. Do you know who stands before you?

FAUSTUS. Should I? Does such a thing warrant a name?

MEPHISTOPHELES. Mark me well, for I am Mephistopheles, and I could offer you such powers no mortal has possessed.

FAUSTUS. I would not have any powers you would gift me. Call your master. Say Faustus would speak with him.

MEPHISTOPHELES. He answers to no one.

FAUSTUS. He shall to me. He must. Do you hear me, Devil? I have come too far – given too much. Out with him!

Now LUCIFER (*played by the same actor who plays* THOMAS) *arrives quietly before her. He wears a cloak and a plague mask.*

Finally. Morning Star. The Shining One.

LUCIFER. Greetings, Faustus.

FAUSTUS. Greetings, Lucifer.

LUCIFER *removes his mask.* FAUSTUS *sees him. She is taken aback.*

Why do you wear my father's face?

LUCIFER. You look to be provided for.

FAUSTUS. No.

LUCIFER. No?

FAUSTUS. No, you will answer my questions then be gone. That is all.

LUCIFER. Talk with me a while. You have impressed me, Faustus.

FAUSTUS. No. My mother –

LUCIFER. Not many I come to.

FAUSTUS. Did you come to her?

LUCIFER. Not many with such drive – such fire. And so little
you've been able to do with it – until now.

FAUSTUS. Did she…? You have a book, don't you – you
keep a book – a list of every wretch who ever gave
themselves to you?

LUCIFER. I do.

FAUSTUS. Is she in it? (*Beat.*) My mother – is she – ?

LUCIFER. None may see it except those who sign it, I'm afraid.

FAUSTUS. But…

She hesitates. MEPHISTOPHELES *laughs.*

What then? What if I signed? Then I could look through it
freely?

MEPHISTOPHELES. Then your immortal soul forever would
be his.

FAUSTUS. But I'd know.

LUCIFER. You would.

FAUSTUS. Then what's a soul? That's little cost to me.

MEPHISTOPHELES. Why, do you have no fear to enter Hell?

FAUSTUS. Why this is Hell, nor am I out of it.
Walk you these streets and say this is not Hell?
See you these souls and say they are not damned?
Live you as I, and do the things I've done,
To daily be debased, and beg for scraps,
To know your talent far outstripped your means,
But for your sex and lowly parentage
Were lost before you even drew a breath?
The Devil take me then.

LUCIFER. If that's your will.

FAUSTUS. And signing I might keep my will my own?
    Why then how could that fate be any worse
    Than to be bound to any common man?
    Oh, if you knew the lives we women lead
    You'd understand the Devil is a catch.

LUCIFER. Then we must have you sign.

FAUSTUS. But not so fast. What else?

LUCIFER. What else?

FAUSTUS. If I am to... I sign, my soul is yours, I'll read your
    book, but that cannot be all.

LUCIFER. So tell me, Faustus, what do you desire?

FAUSTUS. I... (*Thinks.*) To be my own. What do I need for
    that? Time, and space, and... means.

LUCIFER. Go on.

FAUSTUS. Gift me nothing, only opportunity. First, I'll need
    a long and healthy life – impervious to disease – immune
    to hurt.

LUCIFER. Twelve years.

FAUSTUS. Only twelve?

LUCIFER. That's time enough.

FAUSTUS. No – make it twelve times twelve. Twelve times
    twelve and I'll not age a day. Twelve times twelve where
    I shall be all but immortal. And grant me this, that I could
    take those years when I choose, so I might skip through the
    centuries, shrug off millennia, master over time itself – so
    I could set in place the work of a thousand lifetimes, plant
    a seed and walk amongst the forest that springs from it.

MEPHISTOPHELES. She doesn't ask for much.

FAUSTUS. If it's more than he can grant let him say so. (*Back
    to* LUCIFER.) One hundred and forty-four years. What's
    that? Nothing in the face of eternity.

LUCIFER. This we could grant, but only forward. Race toward
the future as you please, but what has passed is past, and
always must stay so.

FAUSTUS. I couldn't visit her – my mother? Save her – let her
speak more? Not even once – just once to – ?

LUCIFER. No.

FAUSTUS. But all this was to… (*Beat.*) No. It was to know –
it was to be certain whether she… I consent. I'd still consent.
(*Beat.*) I'd need some power too.

MEPHISTOPHELES. Here it comes.

FAUSTUS. Power enough to be in the thrall of no man – not so
long as I live. And you may have my soul but not my
servitude. I am my own master. I must have the means to
carry out my will, do you understand?

LUCIFER. Take him.

Beat.

FAUSTUS. What?

LUCIFER. You must have someone. He is a most eligible devil.
So, take Mephistopheles and use him as you will – his
powers yours to command, his knowledge freely shared,
always obedient, for whatever you may wish.

FAUSTUS. I wish to stand alone.

MEPHISTOPHELES. Let her fall alone too.

LUCIFER (*to* FAUSTUS). This is a good match.

FAUSTUS. I need no match. Grant me his powers. I am enough.

LUCIFER. Those are the terms I offer. The choice is yours.

FAUSTUS. He cannot refuse me – or do me harm?

LUCIFER. He can do nothing except that which you bid him do.

FAUSTUS. I… I could consent.

MEPHISTOPHELES. I am not –

LUCIFER (*ignoring* MEPHISTOPHELES, *to* FAUSTUS). And to what comes after? Consent that when the clock strikes twelve at the end of the twelfth month of your final year you shall spend an eternity below?

FAUSTUS. With all this as you've promised?

LUCIFER. All as we've agreed.

FAUSTUS. I could. Good Lord forgive me, but I could.
Yet I could still repent, and yet be saved,
Endure with patience on this bitter earth
And for that earn my place in Paradise.
It's not too late! The church would have me still.
But isn't that the scam – to keep us meek
With promises that we'll inherit much?
Why must we suffer for the life to come?
For I could not be good yet still be great.

LUCIFER. That's the spirit.

FAUSTUS. And yet forever damned…

LUCIFER. Take comfort, Faustus, and know you are damned already.

FAUSTUS. Not yet.

LUCIFER. Sinner since your birth.

FAUSTUS. Not so.

LUCIFER. Your father sees it. You were always ours.

FAUSTUS. I am my own.

LUCIFER. Always. Let me show you.

LUCIFER *puts his hand to* FAUSTUS*'s forehead, which seems to somehow possess her. She cries out, jerking backwards, now channelling each of the seven deadly sins as they tear their way through her. They speed up as they go, building and building. It's painful and horrifying to her, mostly because she knows the truth of it.*

FAUSTUS. Faustus the glutton, never satisfied,
   A sticky-fingered, grasping, fat-cheeked child
   Snapped branches seeking out the sweetest fruit
   And drank, and drank, and drank, and drank, and drank.

   Faustus the lazy, sulking, sullen youth,
   Who only studied spite and scornful looks
   Wasted her days in slothful indolence
   And squandered any wits she might've had.

   Faustus the proud, who thinks herself so great,
   And all around her hapless imbeciles
   Who therefore cannot hope to care or trust
   Who therefore has no hope of being loved.

   Faustus the lustful, wanton, unashamed,
   Who takes her pleasure any way she can
   Who all too cheaply gives herself away
   Who opens legs so they might open doors.

   Faustus the greedy, scrabbling for coin,
   Who only acts if she should stand to gain
   Who turns away the sick if they can't pay
   And mocks the thought of Christian charity.

   Faustus the envious, full of green-eyed bile,
   Watches the menfolk in their finery
   And thinks 'What could I do if I had that?'
   Who deems all undeserving but herself.

   Faustus the wrathful, angry above all,
   Who has such violence coursing through her veins
   A drop of it would set this earth on fire,
   Who is not seeking answers but revenge.

   Admit it, Faustus, this is who you are
   Admit it, Faustus, daughter of the witch
   Admit it, Faustus, you were always damned
   Embodiment of every mortal sin.

   *She is released/the possession ends. She falls to the ground,
   exhausted, drained, panting.*

   What was that?

LUCIFER. That is who you are.

FAUSTUS. No.

MEPHISTOPHELES. Dare you deny it?

FAUSTUS. No! Not damned! Not yet! Not irredeemable!

MEPHISTOPHELES. Wasn't it clear?

FAUSTUS. The Devil's known for tricks. I could spurn you still.

FAUSTUS *glances down at her arm and gasps out.*

MEPHISTOPHELES. What now?

FAUSTUS. No…

LUCIFER. What do you see?

FAUSTUS. See where the blood runs down my arm? I looked just now, and I could swear it spelt out my mother's name.

MEPHISTOPHELES. Oh?

FAUSTUS. What does that mean? Run? Save yourself? Think of her who cared for you? Or does she mean press on? For what was all this for if not for her? You came this far so you might learn the truth, and cannot be dissuaded at the last. She means for me to sign.

MEPHISTOPHELES. Wise mother.

FAUSTUS. I am resolved. A wretched thing I am, but this I'll do. I'll sign.

LUCIFER. As you wish it.

LUCIFER *produces a small leather-bound book from his pocket.*

FAUSTUS. Is that it?

LUCIFER *nods.*

So small.

LUCIFER (*handing her a quill*). In blood, if you will.

FAUSTUS *takes it and, trembling, uses the blood from her arm to make her mark.*

Farewell, Faustus. We'll speak again when the clock strikes twelve.

LUCIFER *turns and goes.* FAUSTUS *sits and begins frantically searching through the pages of the book.*

FAUSTUS. I don't see her.

MEPHISTOPHELES. Who?

FAUSTUS (*with a dawning joy*). She... She isn't here! He doesn't have her! (*Laughs.*) I knew it – I knew she'd never... My mother never signed her name, she never spoke with the Devil. Never did any of it.

MEPHISTOPHELES. No.

FAUSTUS. I'd wager none of them did, who were hung all the same.

MEPHISTOPHELES. I'd wager so.

FAUSTUS. Small comfort. No, great comfort I'd say, to know they're spared from an eternal Hell. Eternal Hell. (*Beat – it hits her.*) Faustus, what've you done?

MEPHISTOPHELES *chuckles.*

I had to know. I had to be certain. (*Beat.*) Does that mean she is...?

MEPHISTOPHELES. Somewhere beyond our reach. Outside my jurisdiction.

FAUSTUS. I can never – ?

MEPHISTOPHELES. No.

FAUSTUS (*after a pause*). Good. Good that she's... I'm glad. Happy.

Silence.

MEPHISTOPHELES. So then.

FAUSTUS. So.

MEPHISTOPHELES *sits beside her.*

MEPHISTOPHELES. Chin up. All done.

FAUSTUS. Yes.

MEPHISTOPHELES. What now?

FAUSTUS. I don't know. Twenty years, wondering if… But now I know.

MEPHISTOPHELES. Yes. Your mother, pure as the driven snow, and how the angels wept to receive her. How far the apple fell.

FAUSTUS. Don't.

MEPHISTOPHELES. Embrace it. Think what you might do now.

FAUSTUS. Yes.

MEPHISTOPHELES. Smile then. It's a great gift you've been given.

FAUSTUS. Damnation?

MEPHISTOPHELES. Liberty.

FAUSTUS. Have you been with Lucifer long?

MEPHISTOPHELES. Ever since the Fall.

FAUSTUS. And why did you rebel?

MEPHISTOPHELES. Because he promised us light.

FAUSTUS. Yes. (*Beat.*) But you failed.

MEPHISTOPHELES. No.

FAUSTUS. He failed you.

MEPHISTOPHELES. No!

FAUSTUS. And you were both punished – you suffer for it still. (*Beat.*) What is your existence now? Tell me honestly.

MEPHISTOPHELES. One of never-ending torments.

FAUSTUS. And would you do it again?

MEPHISTOPHELES. I would.

FAUSTUS. Of course you would. Because there is nothing worse than to spend a lifetime watching others walking around in the light that was meant for you.

MEPHISTOPHELES. Don't suppose to know me, Faustus.

FAUSTUS. I understand you well enough.

MEPHISTOPHELES. You could never –

FAUSTUS. Others – others would say you chose poorly, you were weak or wicked, but I know you had no choice at all. I'd say it's noble – a noble thing to risk everything in the hope the light might fall on you.

MEPHISTOPHELES. We are not the same.

FAUSTUS. No. I am now your master. Your mistress. I don't intend to be a cruel one, but nor shall you forget it.

MEPHISTOPHELES (*biting his tongue*). No, ma'am.

FAUSTUS. You love him still? (*Beat.*) I see you do. Yet he gave you away like it was nothing.

MEPHISTOPHELES. One hundred and forty-four years shall pass in the blink of an eye.

FAUSTUS. He has a thousand others like you, I suppose.

MEPHISTOPHELES. None like me.

FAUSTUS. Poor, pitiable thing you are – both of us abandoned –

MEPHISTOPHELES. I have not –

FAUSTUS. Both alone –

MEPHISTOPHELES. You have no idea! You are my assignment, nothing more. You are still mortal, blessed with temporary gifts. I am as a god to you –

FAUSTUS. You are as nothing, and I answer to no one –

MEPHISTOPHELES. But you shall.

FAUSTUS. No man stands in dominion over me – and none shall ever again. That is my victory – that was the deal I struck.

MEPHISTOPHELES. You know you could be one, if you wanted.

FAUSTUS (*thrown*). What?

MEPHISTOPHELES. A man – should you desire it. I could transform you. The magic is simple enough.

FAUSTUS. Why should I desire that?

MEPHISTOPHELES. Might solve all your problems. Might find it an easier ride. You might even enjoy it.

FAUSTUS. My flesh is not the part at fault.

MEPHISTOPHELES. As you wish.

FAUSTUS. So little ambition.

MEPHISTOPHELES. How's that?

FAUSTUS. Why change my form, when I could change the world it sits in?

MEPHISTOPHELES. That's better. How?

FAUSTUS. All this was for her – all for nothing if it could happen again. It can't happen again. (*Beat.*) I can see it.

MEPHISTOPHELES. See what?

FAUSTUS. The light. That glorious light. We'll have it yet.

They go.

Scene Eight

London, 1665.

Back at the home of DOCTOR NEWBURY, *in the basement. Masked and cloaked* FIGURES *enter,* NEWBURY *is one of them. They also usher on a young* GIRL, *bound, gagged and terrified. They are preparing/beginning some kind of ceremony.* NEWBURY *leads them in a chant. Perhaps he sharpens a knife as he recites.*

NEWBURY. *Diaboli est magna. Lucifer enim magna.*
    Adoramus te, Princeps tenebris
    Non sumus digni, non sumus digni,
    Rex forti, dominus omnium infernum.

    NEWBURY *raises the knife. A figure steps forward, removing their hood. It is* FAUSTUS. *Suddenly* NEWBURY *is the one being bound and* FAUSTUS *holds the knife.*

    Johanna? What is this?

FAUSTUS. I brought you a visitor.

    Another figure lowers his hood. It is MEPHISTOPHELES.

MEPHISTOPHELES. Do you know me, sir?

NEWBURY. Yes! You are the one called Mephistopheles?

MEPHISTOPHELES. The same.

    NEWBURY *laughs in spite of himself.*

FAUSTUS. So you are famous after all?

NEWBURY. Most infamous, and most welcome. Free me. Let us talk.

FAUSTUS. You can talk from there.

NEWBURY (*still to* MEPHISTOPHELES). How did she find you? You never came before – you nor your master.

MEPHISTOPHELES. No.

NEWBURY. Why not?

MEPHISTOPHELES. We found you tedious.

FAUSTUS *laughs*.

NEWBURY. I assure you, we are not. Here I have assembled
some of the greatest minds in Christendom – men of learning
and breeding, wisdom and wickedness –

FAUSTUS. Didn't look like much to me.

NEWBURY (*ignoring this, still to* MEPHISTOPHELES). All
ready to pledge their allegiance to you.

MEPHISTOPHELES. And what would you bid me do?

NEWBURY. Help us rule. Bring kings into our servitude,
queens our courtesans, enslave all who dare defy us and have
the world fall prostrate at our feet. Build me a throne of
golden skulls where I should sit second only to Lucifer, his
right hand, his emissary on Earth.

MEPHISTOPHELES. You see, tedious.

NEWBURY. No, sir.

MEPHISTOPHELES. Yes, you seek to rule, but to what end?

NEWBURY. To… To… What? Is that not ends enough?

MEPHISTOPHELES. To seize a crown so you might wear
      a crown –
So all might call you king, and bow and scrape,
Indulge you in your taste for pageantry –
But what comes next? You know not what you'd do –
You have no itch, no ache, no burning drive –
All your desires are born of idleness –
Yet you dare think you're worthy of our time?

NEWBURY. No. No, you misunderstand –

MEPHISTOPHELES. I know you all too well.

NEWBURY. Yet you would come to her – this wench – this
wretch?

FAUSTUS. Careful, doctor.

NEWBURY. Have you no appetite for greatness?

MEPHISTOPHELES. Only Faustus had potential to be great.

NEWBURY. No – she is nothing. Weak. Worthless. Your master would agree. Ask Lucifer. He shall punish you for this… this insubordination.

MEPHISTOPHELES. Your dissatisfaction has been noted, sir.

NEWBURY (*to* FAUSTUS). You cannot control this beast, but together, we –

FAUSTUS. No, doctor, this is where we part ways. Hold still.

FAUSTUS *unbinds* NEWBURY.

NEWBURY. See reason. After all I did for you –

FAUSTUS (*now with a danger*). Yes, after all you did to me. Don't think I shall leave before you are repaid.

NEWBURY. Now, Johanna –

FAUSTUS. What form of payment should you like?

He realises he has no power here.

NEWBURY. No. Just go. Leave me.

FAUSTUS. With nothing?

NEWBURY. Please. The pleasure was all mine.

FAUSTUS. Yes, I believe it was.

NEWBURY. Remember – you came to me.

FAUSTUS. Yes.

NEWBURY. You were never forced.

FAUSTUS. No.

NEWBURY. But you wanted – you desired –

FAUSTUS. Yes. When I was weak and desperate and in no position to refuse, you bestowed your gifts upon me. Now I should like to do the same. Do you feel able to refuse me, doctor?

NEWBURY. I would receive your gift most graciously.

FAUSTUS. Good. Mephistopheles?

MEPHISTOPHELES *grips* NEWBURY *by the head.*

NEWBURY. But be merciful.

FAUSTUS. Of course. You're a proud devotee of the Devil, are you not?

NEWBURY (*in some pain already*). Yes, Faustus.

FAUSTUS. Then I gift you his horns, so none may doubt where your allegiance lies.

Great spiralling goat horns burst from NEWBURY*'s head.*

And let your hands be fused to cloven hooves, so this poor doctor may do no more harm.

NEWBURY*'s hands are formed into hooves.*

So in this state that best reflects your soul I wish you many years upon this earth, and when they question you on your accursèd form – those who don't scream, or flee, or vomit in disgust – you tell them this: I called forth the Devil, and Faustus answered.

MEPHISTOPHELES. There's someone watching.

FAUSTUS. Who? (*Glances around.*) Come in.

ISABEL, NEWBURY*'s wife, steps forward. She is terrified. She's clearly been watching for a while.*

Good evening, madam.

ISABEL. What have you done?

FAUSTUS. Your husband has had quite the night.

ISABEL. John? What've they…? Change him back.

FAUSTUS. I cannot.

ISABEL. You can.

FAUSTUS. I could, but I choose not to.

ISABEL. Please –

FAUSTUS. This suits him better.

ISABEL. Beg you – release him.

FAUSTUS. I release you.

ISABEL. No – don't do this – you don't have to do this – you
    can stop it.

FAUSTUS. In time you shall thank me.

ISABEL. How are we to live?

FAUSTUS. By your wits, free from his tyranny. Goodnight.

    FAUSTUS *sweeps out,* MEPHISTOPHELES *follows.*
    ISABEL *stares at* NEWBURY.

Scene Nine

The heath, 1665.

ISABEL *comes forward and speaks to us as chorus.*

ISABEL. So Faustus goes, and heads up to the heath
    The night is cool, the moon is bright and high
    And in that moment she feels something

                                        break –

    She is her own.
    Free, for now.
    There is blood fresh in her mouth
    And she likes the taste of it
    Too much
    Conjures wine
    Drinks herself a toast
    And below her the river glitters in the moonlight
    And she does see – a part of her can still see –

The gawping face of his horrified wife
But mostly it's just the doctor
Whose horns shall mark him out always and forever
For the monster that he is
A wounded beast howling in the darkness
A good night's work.
And she smiles
And she drinks
And she can still taste the blood
Is it blood in this bottle?
Is that what the Devil brought her?
She'd drink it anyway
Drink it all down
Rich and thick and intoxicating
And she's thinking, thinking, thinking
And she calls out –

FAUSTUS *and* MEPHISTOPHELES *in the moonlight.*

FAUSTUS. Mephistopheles?

MEPHISTOPHELES. Yes, mistress?

FAUSTUS. Could you help me find them? All of them?

MEPHISTOPHELES. All of who?

FAUSTUS. You know.

MEPHISTOPHELES. I'd need you to say it.

FAUSTUS. All those who spoke against my mother? Who accused her, or gave testimony?

MEPHISTOPHELES. If that was what you wanted. If you commanded.

ISABEL. And they go
Under the cover of night they go
Night after night
For the best part of a year
While her father sleeps
Exhausted by his long and virtuous days.
In the witching hour she finds them –

Mr Hooper
Mr Prentiss
Goody Abbott
Goody Snelling
Judge Gibson
Doctor Collins
The Reverend Fry
All who bore false witness, or spread rumours
Or stood by and said nothing
All who played their part
All will find themselves woken in the dead of night
A figure stood at the end of their bed
A woman with an inscrutable expression
A large black dog at her side
And when they ask –

The JUDGE *appears in a nightgown.*

JUDGE. Who are you?

ISABEL. The figure replies –

FAUSTUS. I am the witch's daughter.

ISABEL. And it was Judge Gibson,
　　He who pronounced the sentence,
　　Who in that moment found courage –

JUDGE. There's no such thing as witches.

　　FAUSTUS *laughs.*

FAUSTUS. So now you know –

ISABEL. Now you know –

　　They speak together.

FAUSTUS/ISABEL. Now you know

　　FAUSTUS *steps towards the* JUDGE. *Lights down.*

Scene Ten

London, 1666.

Late at night. FAUSTUS *has just returned home, fizzing with adrenaline.* THOMAS *is up and fully dressed, waiting for her.* FAUSTUS *spots him and quickly pockets the bloody handkerchief she's been holding.*

FAUSTUS. You're up.

THOMAS. Where have you been?

FAUSTUS. Just taking care of…

THOMAS. Of?

FAUSTUS. I couldn't sleep. I went to see what was growing on the heath.

THOMAS. Alone?

FAUSTUS. I'm careful.

THOMAS. You can't keep disappearing in the middle of the night. Promise me. Promise that you'll – (*Interrupts himself, coughing.*)

FAUSTUS. Are you unwell? Come into the light –

THOMAS. It's nothing.

FAUSTUS. You look like you're burning up – are you – ?

THOMAS. Stay over there.

FAUSTUS. Let me –

THOMAS (*snapping*). You are not to come near me! Do you hear?

Beat.

FAUSTUS. What signs are you showing?

THOMAS. It will pass. It will, but as a precaution… I know of an empty house – empty but uninfected – I'm taking myself away. Just until –

FAUSTUS. I can help you.

THOMAS. I'm taking my bedsheets to burn. I've scrubbed
everything down with vinegar. And I forbid you to follow me
– do you understand?

FAUSTUS. I mean it – I can cure you.

THOMAS. No, Johanna, you cannot.

FAUSTUS. Trust me. Believe me.

THOMAS. Listen – if I don't return –

FAUSTUS. Don't –

THOMAS. Enough! If I am to leave you, at least I'll know...
You've found someone, haven't you?

FAUSTUS (*genuinely thrown*.) What?

THOMAS. I'm not a fool. You aren't really picking flowers on
the heath alone.

FAUSTUS. No.

THOMAS. I've known for some time. I think I've even
glimpsed him once or twice – or just his shadow. Who is he?

FAUSTUS. It's complicated.

THOMAS. Married?

FAUSTUS. No.

THOMAS. Good.

FAUSTUS. He's mine for now, but his heart belongs to another.

THOMAS. I see. The best you might hope for, I suppose. Still,
I'm sorry not to have met him. He can provide for you?

FAUSTUS. I am provided for.

THOMAS. Good. That's good.

FAUSTUS. Please. You needn't go.

THOMAS. I couldn't say what it was, but you have been more
yourself these last few months than I have ever known you.
Finally thriving. Finally content.

FAUSTUS. No, that isn't –

THOMAS. I'm happy for you. Still, be careful when you go
walking in the moonlight.

FAUSTUS. I will.

THOMAS. Stay safe now, and God bless you.

FAUSTUS. Please.

THOMAS *goes. Her instinct is to follow but she stops*
herself. A pause. MEPHISTOPHELES *emerges.*

Could I have stopped this? Could I have done something
more? I had the capacity for greatness – you told me that.

MEPHISTOPHELES. And once you did.

FAUSTUS. Not any more?

MEPHISTOPHELES. No. Now you have the Devil in your
brain. Now you can achieve nothing without having that
worm whisper 'This was all his cunning, not your own.'

FAUSTUS. No. Faustus is still her own.

MEPHISTOPHELES. But your powers are his.

FAUSTUS. And greatness doesn't lie within the sword, but they
who wield it. I may yet be great.

MEPHISTOPHELES. Believe you so?

FAUSTUS. Not good, but still great. What – you think Faustus
too prideful to act, for fear the Devil gets the credit? No,
I may be damned but I am not yet done. I will do *something*.

MEPHISTOPHELES. Like what?

FAUSTUS. Something. Something big. Something to… My
father is sick.

MEPHISTOPHELES. Yes.

FAUSTUS. He shall die.

MEPHISTOPHELES. All shall.

FAUSTUS. But soon?

MEPHISTOPHELES. Didn't sound well, did he?

FAUSTUS. And yet you could...? No. He would rather die
a thousand deaths than be saved by the Devil. All your gifts
lead to damnation, but there must be *something*. Yes, I am
damned – Faustus is damned and that is irrevocable, but
I could stem the flow of blood.

MEPHISTOPHELES. Giving up so soon?

FAUSTUS. No.

MEPHISTOPHELES. No stomach for it.

FAUSTUS. That isn't –

MEPHISTOPHELES. No stamina.

FAUSTUS. More imagination. If there is a worm in my brain it
has been you goading me towards vengeance. But no more.
I have it now. I'll make Lucifer regret his deal. For now we
shall do good; I shall save the world to spite the Devil.

MEPHISTOPHELES. There can be no mercy for you – your
soul is ours.

FAUSTUS. So be it then! For who is better placed to act
selflessly than she who knows she is already damned? What
reason not to give my life in service? My father's motto: 'And
throughout the world I am called the bringer of help.' And my
mother – my mother who knew the name of every plant in the
forest – I'll carry on her work. And that way I'll be great. That
is how I'll have my vengeance. I shall be a doctor to the
world, and you – you shall be my nursemaid. You shall carry
my bags and follow my orders, do you understand?

MEPHISTOPHELES. You are no healer, Faustus. Why deny
yourself?

FAUSTUS. I deny you.

MEPHISTOPHELES. You can do nothing without me.

FAUSTUS. And you must do as I command. The Devil in my
brain cried 'Lay those villains low', but gave no thought to

raising others up – raising *all* up. Healing my father still
won't keep him safe – he shall never rest while this city ails.
But you – you are one of those who has the power to spread
great pestilences, are you not?

MEPHISTOPHELES. I am.

FAUSTUS. And therefore stands to reason you could also
banish them.

MEPHISTOPHELES. Perhaps.

FAUSTUS. Yes or no.

MEPHISTOPHELES. I could.

FAUSTUS. So, we must see what the Devil can really do.
(*Beat*.) Mephistopheles, I command you: rid this city of the
plague. There. You have your instruction. Do it. Do it now.

MEPHISTOPHELES. As you wish.

MEPHISTOPHELES *clicks his fingers. A pause*.

FAUSTUS. Is that it?

MEPHISTOPHELES. It's started.

*Slowly, gradually, the sound of crackling fire builds. Hints of
smoke, and orange light. Soon distant cries and shouting.
All this creeps in by increments under what follows.*

FAUSTUS. How? (*Beat*.) How, Devil?

MEPHISTOPHELES *smiles*.

What have you started?

MEPHISTOPHELES. Your first great work.

FAUSTUS. Tell me. Mephistopheles! What've you done?

MEPHISTOPHELES. What you asked.

FAUSTUS. I never –

We are now clearly aware of the flames building.

MEPHISTOPHELES. A great cleansing fire. The salvation they deserve.

FAUSTUS. No –

MEPHISTOPHELES. Come – come fly over the city with me. See how it spreads, consumes, how all London burns –

FAUSTUS. I didn't – I never...

MEPHISTOPHELES. Grown shy now, Faustus?

FAUSTUS. I can't... No – I can't stay here – I...

MEPHISTOPHELES (*staring into the fire*). Look at the light, Faustus – that glorious light!

Lights out, sound of the fire grows deafening.

End of Act One.

ACT TWO

Scene One

London, 1866.

FAUSTUS *is covered head to toe in a white ash, curled in a ball, in a state of shock. Suddenly she jerks up, fully alert, with a cry.*

FAUSTUS. Fire!

> *She looks around, disorientated.*

> Mephistopheles?

> MEPHISTOPHELES *emerges, immaculate, as always.*

> Water – bring water – conjure... I command you – put this fire out.

MEPHISTOPHELES. The fire is out.

FAUSTUS. Oh. Good. (*Beat.*) Where are we?

MEPHISTOPHELES. London, still.

FAUSTUS. London is still – ?

MEPHISTOPHELES. The city survives.

FAUSTUS. And the plague?

MEPHISTOPHELES. Gone.

> FAUSTUS *laughs weakly, in spite of herself.*

FAUSTUS. You kept your word?

MEPHISTOPHELES. You really should've stayed to watch. Burned most prettily. But those who survived their trial by fire found themselves clean.

FAUSTUS. You tricked me.

MEPHISTOPHELES. Only as you ordered. I am the sword you wield. Mind you don't cut yourself.

FAUSTUS *tries to stand*.

FAUSTUS. I need to see my father.

A pause. MEPHISTOPHELES *smiles*.

No. Don't say you let him burn.

MEPHISTOPHELES. He was nowhere near the fire when it started.

FAUSTUS. But?

MEPHISTOPHELES. Alas. He ran towards the flames – ran to find his daughter, searched high and low. And wept – oh, how he wept when he couldn't find her.

FAUSTUS. Couldn't find me?

MEPHISTOPHELES. Enough, you might think, to quench the burning timbers with his tears, but not enough to save him. Still, he died a Christian death.

FAUSTUS. I meant to help.

MEPHISTOPHELES. What did *you* do when you saw those flames? Run towards them? Call for water? What?

FAUSTUS (*starts to remember*). I ran.

MEPHISTOPHELES. And what did you bid me do?

FAUSTUS. Take me away.

MEPHISTOPHELES. Yes.

FAUSTUS. From all of it. Far away.

MEPHISTOPHELES. How far?

FAUSTUS (*gasps*). Forward.

MEPHISTOPHELES. Yes.

FAUSTUS. I didn't… I panicked.

MEPHISTOPHELES. How far, Faustus?

FAUSTUS (*disbelieving*). Two hundred years. (*Beat.*) And I can't go back?

MEPHISTOPHELES *shakes his head.*

And I did nothing to help them. So that is my true nature. Sinner after all. (*Beat.*) Two hundred years? And London stands. Do I have family here? I must have ancestors, I must –

MEPHISTOPHELES. You are the last of your line.

FAUSTUS. Cousins in the country – in-laws, or –

MEPHISTOPHELES. No one.

FAUSTUS. Not a soul? I looked to stand alone, so… Does he have a grave? My father – does he – ?

MEPHISTOPHELES. None that still stands.

FAUSTUS. I should go join him, I suppose, if I were decent. Before I can do any more damage. (*Genuinely curious.*) Can I die – or am I bound to serve out my full time?

MEPHISTOPHELES. Try it – find out. (*Beat.*) You don't want to die, Faustus – however wretched you become.

FAUSTUS. No.

MEPHISTOPHELES. No. You *are* the fire, and fire has no conscience. It only consumes – transforms – takes hold.

FAUSTUS. Those are your dreams, not mine.

MEPHISTOPHELES. You may not think me a friend, but this world is to us a common enemy. Let's have at it.

FAUSTUS. No.

MEPHISTOPHELES. Or you freed yourself for nothing.

FAUSTUS. I shan't be a tool for your vengeance.

MEPHISTOPHELES. Tick-tock, Faustus – the clock is running down.

FAUSTUS. I have time enough – might I just live for a while?

MEPHISTOPHELES. But with no purpose?

FAUSTUS. I need something to pin me down, before I float away. And then what? Maybe I should like to burn.

DRESSERS *enter and begin to clean up* FAUSTUS *before helping her into a large nineteenth-century dress with full underskirts. Into –*

Scene Two

London, 1866.

A SINGER *appears. While she sings, we see snatches of* FAUSTUS *experiencing nineteenth-century London,* MEPHISTOPHELES *always hovering close by.* FAUSTUS *drinks. She eats expensive things. She sleeps with both men and women. She takes a male lover and dresses in his clothes. She watches bare-knuckle boxing. Maybe she has* MEPHISTOPHELES *beat someone. Maybe she fights herself. She smokes opium. She exists in a haze. She isn't necessarily enjoying herself – perhaps we even get the sense that she is suffering – but she keeps herself occupied. About a year passes in this fashion.*

The song is an extract from a seventeenth-century ballad, 'Death and the Lady'. It should be slow and sad, and a bit trippy. Somewhere between Restoration England and Twin Peaks *jazz.*

SINGER (*sings*). 'Fair Lady, throw those costly robes aside,
    No longer may you glory in your pride;
    Take leave of all your carnal vain delight,
    I'm come to summon you away this night.'

    'What bold attempt is this? Pray let me know
    From whence you come, and whither I must go.
    Shall I, who am a lady, stoop or bow
    To such a pale-faced visage? Who art thou?'

'Do you not know me? I will tell you then:
I am he that conquers all the sons of men,
No pitch of honour from my dart is free,
My name is Death! Have you not heard of me?'

'Yes; I have heard of thee, time after time;
But, being in the glory of my prime,
I did not think you would have come so soon;
Why must my morning sun go down at noon?'

'Why must my morning sun go down at noon?'

The SINGER *goes. A shift. Into –*

Scene Three

London, 1867.

The practice of DOCTOR ELIZABETH GARRETT.
FAUSTUS *is with her, perhaps not entirely sure how she
got here.*

GARRETT. Johanna?

FAUSTUS. Yes.

GARRETT. Please, come through.

FAUSTUS. Thank you.

GARRETT. What appears to be the problem?

FAUSTUS. I'm here to see the doctor.

GARRETT. Yes.

FAUSTUS. Doctor… Garrett, I think? I had an appointment
made.

GARRETT. Yes. (*Beat, then with a sigh.*) Yes, I am she.

FAUSTUS. You're the doctor?

GARRETT. Yes.

FAUSTUS. You?

GARRETT (*testily*). Yes, I am the doctor. Yes, I am a real doctor. No, if you are not interested in my services you are under no compulsion to stay.

FAUSTUS. I...

GARRETT. You had an appointment made?

FAUSTUS. Yes.

GARRETT. But with no knowledge that you would be seeing the first qualified female doctor in England?

FAUSTUS. Yes.

GARRETT. Really?

FAUSTUS. I didn't think to ask.

GARRETT. So – what ails you?

FAUSTUS. I haven't been sleeping.

GARRETT. Anything else? Have you been sick?

FAUSTUS. No, I don't get sick.

GARRETT. We all get sick.

FAUSTUS. Not me.

GARRETT. Then you are blessed.

FAUSTUS. No, not blessed either.

GARRETT. How long has your sleep been disrupted?

FAUSTUS. Ever since... A year, maybe? I lost my father, I... (*A new thought.*) You are the first – the first woman?

GARRETT. On these shores.

FAUSTUS (*more to herself*). Two hundred years!

GARRETT. I'm sorry?

FAUSTUS. It took that long! How did you do it? Where did you train?

GARRETT. With the Guild of Apothecaries.

FAUSTUS *laughs in delight.* GARRETT *stares.*

FAUSTUS. Sorry. My father, he was an apothecary. He would've been amazed.

GARRETT. Of course they changed the rules after – ensured no other woman could follow me, but –

FAUSTUS. So you're the only one?

GARRETT. For now. (*Moving on.*) If you're not sleeping –

FAUSTUS. I once thought I might – follow him in... I was to be a doctor, a professor, scholar, surgeon, scientist, fount of all knowledge –

GARRETT (*laughs*). Were you indeed?

FAUSTUS. Don't laugh at me.

GARRETT. I'm not – I'm sorry.

FAUSTUS. You don't know me. I could still... You have two centuries of advantage – no idea what I might've... Why you?

GARRETT. I had some good fortune, certainly. A natural aptitude, and determination –

FAUSTUS (*a flash of realisation*). No – no, I see it now – of course.

GARRETT. See what?

FAUSTUS. How else could you have done it? No – we're more alike than I realised. How did you find him? What deal did you strike?

GARRETT. Find who?

FAUSTUS. And how long did he promise you – when you signed your name in his book?

GARRETT. What book?

FAUSTUS. Don't worry – I understand! We are hostages to our sex. A wise man has no need for the Devil, but a wise woman knows the Devil is no worse than man.

GARRETT. How long has it been since you last slept?

FAUSTUS. Forget about that.

GARRETT. The strain of sleep deprivation is a very real –

FAUSTUS. No! Don't do this. I'm telling you I *know*! I know why you made your pact, for I did the same! We should stand united.

GARRETT. Let me prescribe you something for your nerves.

FAUSTUS. There is nothing wrong with my nerves! Listen to me – I will speak plainly. My name is Johanna Faustus. I was born over two hundred years ago. I gave my soul to achieve the impossible. I watched this city grow sick and I swore to heal it. But I was weak. I watched it burn and then I fled. But now… I know what you gave – to sign over your soul to the Devil –

GARRETT. I do not believe in the Devil, madam.

FAUSTUS. You had to.

GARRETT. I believe in science. I believe in hard work and perseverance. I believe a woman can achieve anything she sets her mind to, and yes, she requires luck and intelligence and resourcefulness, but not… diabolic interference.

FAUSTUS. No –

GARRETT. And our position is precarious. Our place hard-won. For every door we prise open three more are nailed shut. But still we battle on.

FAUSTUS (*now she falters*). You really did all this yourself?

GARRETT. Not alone. Not without friends, without sisters –

FAUSTUS. But you never called him? Lucifer? Beelzebub? Mephistopheles?

GARRETT. I'm sorry I spoke to you sharply. I would like to find you a room at Bedlam. They have fine rooms – private rooms – not like the stories you hear.

FAUSTUS. I… I…

GARRETT. Purely so you can recuperate – sleep – rest.

FAUSTUS. No.

GARRETT. If you have a little money they will treat you kindly.

FAUSTUS. I'm not… I'm sorry. Forgive me.

GARRETT. You have nothing to be forgiven for.

FAUSTUS. Not so.

GARRETT. Please, sit – I have the time. You have seen things – visions? You believe the Devil has come to you?

FAUSTUS. I'm stupid.

GARRETT. Not at all. Without sleep –

Suddenly FAUSTUS *flings her arms around* GARRETT. GARRETT *doesn't know how to respond.*

Please –

FAUSTUS. You didn't need him. It was all you.

GARRETT. I'm going to get you help.

FAUSTUS. No, you've done enough. (*Releases* GARRETT.) You won't remember this – I couldn't live with the shame of you remembering – but I will. Thank you, doctor.

FAUSTUS *steps away and* GARRETT *goes. Straight into –*

Scene Four

London, 1867.

FAUSTUS *has come straight from her appointment with* GARRETT.

FAUSTUS. So, she is who I might've been.

MEPHISTOPHELES *appears.*

The better self I never now can be – not with this worm in my brain, Devil on my shoulder, sickness at my core.

MEPHISTOPHELES. Weren't you inspired?

FAUSTUS. I haven't been unkind to you of late. I have embraced the sinner in me – indulged every impulse – allowed you your pleasures too. Why am I being punished?

MEPHISTOPHELES. Oh, Faustus, this is not your punishment.

FAUSTUS. And she must've had... Two hundred years – and wealth – privilege, surely? All the trappings of –

MEPHISTOPHELES. No.

FAUSTUS. No?

MEPHISTOPHELES. So what's to be done? Shall we break her fingers? Send her mad? Teach her a lesson for achieving all that Faustus sought?

FAUSTUS. No!

MEPHISTOPHELES. Or you could replace her – wear her face a while, until you tire of it. Slice her to pieces so you might practise her art.

FAUSTUS. Stop it!

MEPHISTOPHELES. Then what?

FAUSTUS. I don't know!

MEPHISTOPHELES. 'I don't know!' Oh, you are such a disappointment! Find your ambition! Humans sin with no help from the Devil, but you came to Lucifer to be *freed*.

You saw the natural order was not in fact natural at all and
you would overthrow it. So if I bring you to a woman who
has done remarkable things with naught but the grace of God
– (*Spits*.) then what more might you do?

FAUSTUS. Leave me.

MEPHISTOPHELES. Coward. *Do* something.

FAUSTUS. No! You would goad me towards another disaster.

MEPHISTOPHELES. Kill or cure, the world must be
transformed.

FAUSTUS. And what can I do here? Two hundred years and
she is still the only one – oh, the pace of progress is so slow!
I could jump forward – another hundred years, two hundred,
a thousand –

MEPHISTOPHELES. Name the date.

FAUSTUS. Yet still she did it here – Garrett did it here. She sets
a path and clears the way for all others who come after.
Should I stay?

MEPHISTOPHELES. Take action.

FAUSTUS. Not blindly. I must be certain, I... (*A decision*.)
I must study.

MEPHISTOPHELES. What do you seek to know?

FAUSTUS. I seek to learn. I am starved of education but
blessed with time. Take me to a library – there with your
magic pick their locks, nothing more.

MEPHISTOPHELES. Knowledge is not enough.

FAUSTUS. It's a start.

MEPHISTOPHELES. Your merits shall never be enough – not
as things are. Why pick a lock when you could burn the
palace down? Be bold. Light a fire. Let us peel the flesh from
the bones of every man who thinks women inferior, so they
may see their skeletons are alike.

FAUSTUS. No.

MEPHISTOPHELES. Wouldn't that be virtuous, in your eyes?

FAUSTUS. Then you would not encourage it.

MEPHISTOPHELES. I only have an itch to spread my wings.
Unleash me, Faustus. Let me be a scythe for your justice.

FAUSTUS. Not yet. I am resolute. I must lay roots. Who else
can plant seeds and live to see the forest grown? Only when
I know all of this age might I leave it. Only when I am
certain might I act. I have much to learn.

Scene ends. Into –

Scene Five

GARRETT *speaks to us as chorus. We see* FAUSTUS *studying.*

GARRETT. True to her word, Faustus takes to her books
    Much to the Devil's disappointment
    And spends her days in earnest study,
    Furrowed brows and furious concentration
    And finds... And finds much of it to be deeply tedious
    Spends whole weeks staring at a single sentence
    Mephistopheles hovering over her shoulder
    Who could make all of this so much more *fun*,
    She feels the fire crackling within her,
    Itching to be unleashed
    But she is stubborn
    Keeps herself honest just to spite him
    And in time what was a chore becomes a pleasure
    She reads for ten years
    Barely stopping for sustenance or conversation
    And by the time she's done there are more books to read,
    So she takes to her library again
    And now conducts experiments
    Pursuing strange new forms of healing
    Where science and fantasy converge
    Mourns that she missed Mary Shelley –

FAUSTUS. Damn.

GARRETT. And Mary Wollstonecraft.

FAUSTUS. Damn!

GARRETT. And Enlightenment as a whole –

> FAUSTUS *sighs, her head slumping on her desk.*

Typical, just typical
That the world only flourished when she left it.
No matter. Now she visits colleges, universities,
Finds not all doors are open to her
But enough – enough for now –
Enough for her to get started
Uses Mephistopheles only to pay her fees
Completes one degree, hops continents
And completes another, just to be sure.
In this manner almost thirty years pass,
Though she hasn't aged a day.
Adds the title of doctor to her name – no short cuts –
And swears her oath:

FAUSTUS *and* GARRETT. *Primum non nocere* –

FAUSTUS. First, do no harm.

GARRETT. And it is this promise – this solemn vow –
That will keep her hands firmly bound
Her studies theoretical, the world at arm's length,
For she is still the Devil's instrument.
Even so, as a new century dawns
Johanna Faustus is the wisest woman in Europe
Laboratories buzz with talk of her genius
But she will take no credit,
And adjusts awkwardly to this ill-fitting coat of modesty.
Still, she has her own people now –
People she forbids Mephistopheles to meet.
And she is building up to something –
To the day she puts theory into action –
Soon – it will be soon.

GARRETT *goes.*

Scene Six

London, 1903.

FAUSTUS *is entertaining* MARIE CURIE *(thirty-six) and* PIERRE CURIE *(forty-four) in her London home. It's late evening. Wine has been drunk. The* CURIES *are dressed smartly but not ostentatiously, having been honoured at the Royal Institution.* FAUSTUS *is the most relaxed we've seen her.*

FAUSTUS. Another bottle?

MARIE. Not for me.

FAUSTUS. Are you sure? Pierre? You've earned it.

PIERRE. I'll be sick.

FAUSTUS. Then eat more too – line your stomach. I know those dinners – the richer the guests the smaller the portions.

MARIE. Rich enough, for sure. Some of their jewels –

PIERRE *(to* FAUSTUS). Marie and I kept whispering to each other – with that brooch we could build a new laboratory.

FAUSTUS. Steal a couple when you're back tomorrow.

PIERRE. I'd sooner stay here in bed.

MARIE. But you were brilliant tonight.

PIERRE. I was a fool. *(To* FAUSTUS.) Wracked with nerves – my hands trembling. I spilled radium all over the hall – did you hear?

MARIE. It's not your fault – the way your hands are.

PIERRE. Yes.

FAUSTUS. Can I see them?

PIERRE. It's nothing. But another reason not to be trusted with red wine. *(To* MARIE.) I never should've agreed in the first place. I should've refused to speak unless you were there beside me.

MARIE. I was still championed. *(To* FAUSTUS.) He spent as much time singing my praises as he did talking about science.

PIERRE. I merely gave credit where it's due.

FAUSTUS (*to* MARIE). Absurd, the way you're treated.

MARIE. I have my allies. If Magnus hadn't written to us – and Pierre hadn't put his foot down – I would've never been nominated alongside him. The first husband in recorded history to insist his wife shares his spoils. Johanna, wouldn't you say I have the finest husband in recorded history?

FAUSTUS. Is there much competition?

MARIE. I am blessed to have extraordinary men in my corner.

FAUSTUS. No – they are blessed to know you!

PIERRE. Amen.

FAUSTUS (*to* MARIE). They gift you nothing by – by what? – by allowing your efforts to be recognised? That is not a favour – that should not be extraordinary. You elevate them. Your work makes them appear more than they are, and you are *thankful* for it?

MARIE. I am permitted to be.

PIERRE. No, I agree. You know what they say at the university? They say 'Pierre Curie – his greatest discovery is his wife.' No argument from me.

MARIE. You see – the finest husband in recorded history.

PIERRE *and* MARIE *kiss.* FAUSTUS *looks away.* MARIE *chuckles.*

Oh, don't pull that face.

FAUSTUS. Sorry – I'm sorry. And I meant nothing personal, Pierre.

PIERRE. I know.

FAUSTUS (*to* MARIE). But don't you see you should need no champions? And not have to feel grateful when you're given some small portion of your due.

PIERRE. Hear, hear.

MARIE. Yes – continue to lecture me, Johanna Faustus, about the importance of claiming my place, when you won't put your name on a single paper – give public lectures – take up a professorship –

FAUSTUS. The universities are queuing up, are they, to induct female professors?

MARIE. That isn't the point.

PIERRE (*to* FAUSTUS). If you desired it – any introduction I could make –

FAUSTUS. No. Thank you.

MARIE. Why not? Surely your example –

FAUSTUS. Who needs Johanna Faustus when they have Marie Curie?

MARIE. Excuses.

FAUSTUS. I don't require it.

MARIE. But the things you do –

PIERRE. Don't needle her.

MARIE. She started it. (*To* FAUSTUS.) I have seen you work miracles – no field of modern science not somehow indebted to your thinking. They should be building statues of you – teaching you in every school. Galileo, Newton, Faustus – why shouldn't – ?

FAUSTUS (*too sudden, too strong*). No! Do not tempt me! (*Beat. Stops herself. Tries to laugh it off.*) I'm not... Sorry.

MARIE. No, I'm sorry. I didn't...

FAUSTUS. The wine, I...

PIERRE. We're all tired.

MARIE. Yes.

FAUSTUS. But I cannot... I sought that kind of greatness once, when I was young –

PIERRE. You're still young. (*To* MARIE.) Johanna doesn't age
– have you noticed that?

MARIE. That's how a woman ages without children.

PIERRE. Ah, yes.

FAUSTUS. But anything that bears my name shall be tainted
by it.

MARIE. Why?

FAUSTUS. Please, just believe me when I say it is. Let me do
my work in peace and quiet. Let me try to do good, much
though I struggle with it.

MARIE. I don't understand.

PIERRE. But we respect you, all the same. (*Drawing a line*.)
I think I might be heading towards bed – I slept so little
last night.

FAUSTUS. Yes, yes.

> PIERRE *kisses* MARIE.

PIERRE. Don't stay up too late.

MARIE. No, I shan't be far behind.

> PIERRE *goes*.

FAUSTUS. He's sick?

MARIE. Works too hard – we both do.

FAUSTUS. But the work must be done.

MARIE. Yes.

FAUSTUS. I wanted to talk to you about radium.

MARIE. It's late.

FAUSTUS. We used to stay up all hours – wouldn't sleep,
wouldn't eat –

MARIE. Before Pierre – before Irène –

FAUSTUS. Holding you back.

MARIE. No.

FAUSTUS. At least you only have the one.

MARIE *looks away.*

You're not...? (*Off* MARIE*'s look*.) Any fool can have a child, Marie – the gifts you have are rare.

MARIE. You're being cruel.

FAUSTUS. Honest. Without them –

MARIE. I would be nowhere. When Pierre saw the work I was doing he abandoned his own projects to join mine –

FAUSTUS. Yes – he hitched his fortunes to your brilliance –

MARIE. No –

FAUSTUS. So now what might have been yours alone is yours together.

MARIE. And together is not worse!

FAUSTUS. It is weaker.

MARIE. No. We are a team. Every tedious, mundane hour is made bearable because he is by my side. If you had someone, Johanna –

FAUSTUS. There's no match out there for me.

MARIE. Why do you seek to heal the world when you have such disdain for it?

FAUSTUS. Because I can. (*Beat.*) Now, radium –

MARIE. Goodnight, Johanna.

FAUSTUS. You used to keep a jar of it beside your bed as a nightlight – do you still do that?

MARIE. Sometimes.

FAUSTUS. You know there's magic in it – near enough. Magic merely science we don't understand. I think it might be the answer to something.

MARIE. To what?

FAUSTUS. Immortality.

MARIE *laughs*. FAUSTUS *doesn't*.

MARIE. You're serious?

FAUSTUS. When we have cured all disease we shall have cured death, for there will be nothing left to take us – that is the logical endpoint of the path we're on.

MARIE. That is fantasy.

FAUSTUS. Perhaps. Do you remember *Frankenstein*?

MARIE. The monster story?

FAUSTUS. A story, yes, but with science at its heart. Shelley hypothesised – almost one hundred years ago – that under the right circumstances a dead body might have life restored to it. But how? We know – we can demonstrate – that the right electric charge can mimic some characteristics of life. We know – through Pierre's electrometer – how to measure electric charge with greater precision than ever before. And we know that radium emits energy – in the form of rays, yes – giving out heat and light, and – miraculously – it has the capacity to *heal* – it attacks diseased tissue and leaves healthy cells intact. So – so what if this strange, new and impossible element was in fact that mythological substance alchemists have sought for a thousand years – our very own Philosopher's Stone?

MARIE. You can't believe any of this.

FAUSTUS. And what if at the moment of our demise the spirit departs, but we could then reanimate the body to live on? Live free from the tyranny of our souls?

MARIE. And if you did believe in such a thing as the soul, why on earth should you desire to live without one?

FAUSTUS. Oh, I have long sought to be rid of mine.

MARIE. That is the wine talking.

FAUSTUS. Let it burn forever below, while I remain here, untroubled – my mind still thinking, my body still working, free from judgement or censure – wouldn't that be a remarkable thing?

MARIE. I'm going to bed.

FAUSTUS. All will be possible, in time.

MARIE. You're brilliant, Johanna, but you're overtired. Get some rest.

FAUSTUS. I won't sleep. I have too much to do.

MARIE *goes. Into –*

Scene Seven

The SINGER *returns, and we get another verse of 'Death and the Lady'. Perhaps we see* FAUSTUS *continue to work through this. We also get our first glimpse of the three horsemen,* WAR, FAMINE *and* PESTILENCE, *starting to gather, though we don't know who they are yet. These are sinister, possibly masked and not-wholly-human figures, who seem rooted in the seventeenth century.*

SINGER. (*sings*) 'Ye learnèd doctors, now exert your skill,
  And let not Death on me obtain his will!
  Prepare your cordials, let me comfort find,
  My gold shall fly like chaff before the wind!'

  'Forbear to call! That skill will never do;
  They are but mortals here as well as you.
  I give the fatal wound, my dart is sure,
  And far beyond the doctors' skill to cure.

  And far beyond the doctors' skill to cure.'

The SINGER *goes.*

Scene Eight

London, 1903.

FAUSTUS *and* MEPHISTOPHELES. FAUSTUS *has a letter.*
The HORSEMEN *linger in the shadows.*

FAUSTUS. She lost her baby. Marie.

MEPHISTOPHELES. Yes. Will you visit her in Paris?

FAUSTUS. No. No, she'll be of no use to me for a while.
(*Beat.*) She couldn't see it.

MEPHISTOPHELES. See what?

FAUSTUS. The real prize. A world without sickness is a worthy
goal, but a world without *death*? That is the one true
liberation. Without death the threshold into Heaven or Hell is
never crossed, therefore we need not please God or fear the
Devil – we are finally our *own* – we are sovereign – there is
no one above us. Isn't that the revolution you once sought?

MEPHISTOPHELES. He will still come for you.

FAUSTUS. I know. And I'll be ready. But I cannot do it here.
Electricity still in its infancy, machine computing languishes,
new elements we barely understand. I have a little over a
hundred years left to stretch throughout all of time and I am
tired! Tired of this age! It sickens me. Marie Curie shall soon
have a Nobel Prize yet still she cannot vote. I can't stay here.

MEPHISTOPHELES. You won't take up arms, then? Bravely
join the fight for suffrage?

FAUSTUS. I can't.

MEPHISTOPHELES. Faustus the saviour – Faustus the great
redeemer?

FAUSTUS. What, with you as my lieutenant? No. No, I would
bring them disaster. I cannot walk the Devil into their houses.

MEPHISTOPHELES. So the good doctor will keep her hands
clean.

FAUSTUS. I will help. I promise I will help, but... They shall triumph without me, and no one else can do what I do – plant a seed and walk amongst the forest.

MEPHISTOPHELES. As you wish.

FAUSTUS. One hundred years. We'll keep a lookout – never too far at once – observe, adapt, move on. But I need the data. I need the technology. I need the world to catch up with me. I'm ready – I'll be ready.

FAUSTUS *smiles. Into –*

Scene Nine

A shift. A rumble. Things are starting to come apart. We see a hundred years of science and medicine pass. We see nuclear fission. We see the atom bomb. We see cells divide under microscopes. We see diseases cured. We see chemical weapons. We see DNA being modified. We see the Large Hadron Collider. FAUSTUS *watches all of this with us – a complete sensory overload. She is horrified and delighted. During this sequence she is also dressed in smart, twenty-first-century business attire. Into –*

Scene Ten

London. 2036.

Our travelling-through-time sequence segues into a corporate video. We see lots of glossy, abstract science footage, suitably slick and arty, a Terrence Malick-perfume-commercial vibe. We begin tranquil/reflective and gradually pick up pace as the video continues. Over this we hear a deeply earnest VOICE-OVER.

VOICE-OVER. Where are we?
How did we get here?
Who put us here, and why?
When I woke up the world was burning
We watched the smoke signals
And they told us
Things couldn't go on like this
We had failed
We had been judged
We had been found wanting
But now…
Now I understand…

We start to pick up speed.

What if the fire was clearing the way for something?
Something bigger, better, brighter
Something new
Something that would transform us
And prepare us for the days ahead
The world is changing
Our challenges are new challenges
Our opportunities are new opportunities
And there is only one thing that can save us –

On this cue, the word 'YOU' appears in huge letters.

You.

The legend 'YOU CAN CHANGE' fills the space, alongside a logo for the Institute.

The Faustus Institute: You Can Change.

FAUSTUS *enters to applause. She addresses the audience as if they are a new intake of staff members at some training seminar. The feel is clean, bright and expensive. We might now see some sort of TED Talk-style visual aids accompanying her talk.*

FAUSTUS. How many angels can dance on the head of a pin? You know this one? It's not a joke, it's an old, old question – one that's preoccupied philosophers and theologians for centuries. Now, there isn't an answer – the point is that there isn't an answer – but I've been thinking about it a lot, because it is, in some ways, one of the most fundamental questions of computing. How much and how small. How much data can we cram into any given space? How can we shrink it down? How many angels, and how big is your pin?

The first computer filled a room – we all know that. Your smartphone has more processing power than the set-up that put man on the moon. So what's next? Let's think big – or really small.

The human brain contains about one hundred terabytes of data – ballpark figure. And y'know, these days, that's not so much. Data capture – mind-mapping – the creation of an online consciousness – that is no longer science-fiction, that is a scientific inevitability – that is, I believe, the next step of our evolution. So that's what you're going to be working on. E-LXR. Digital immortality. That's where we're all heading. Let's get to work.

She smiles broadly. Lights shift and FAUSTUS *is joined by* MEPHISTOPHELES. FAUSTUS*'s nose is bleeding.*

So? What do you think of our new recruits?

MEPHISTOPHELES. All highly qualified. (*Gesturing to* FAUSTUS*'s nose.*) You might want to –

FAUSTUS. Oh, shit.

She wipes her nose with a tissue.

MEPHISTOPHELES. And you wanted the land survey for the DRC site?

FAUSTUS. Thanks. We need conflict-free copper. Zero exploitation. Is Yolanda down there?

MEPHISTOPHELES. Yes.

FAUSTUS. Good.

MEPHISTOPHELES. You know you do only have to ask. If you need copper, I can bring you copper. If you want diamonds I'll get you diamonds. If you want the toenail clippings of Cleopatra –

FAUSTUS. Isaac Newton.

MEPHISTOPHELES. You want Isaac Newton?

FAUSTUS. For every action, an equal and opposite reaction. Even if I try to use you for good –

MEPHISTOPHELES. You have at your command a creature with near unlimited supernatural gifts, and you use me as your secretary.

FAUSTUS. Don't be hard on yourself – you're an Executive Assistant. (*Moving on.*) When does Helen get back?

MEPHISTOPHELES. Around eight – but the Supreme Court won't budge on human trials.

FAUSTUS. We'll see.

MEPHISTOPHELES. A little squeamish when your mind-mapping results in 'near-certain fatality'.

FAUSTUS. We have consent. That's why we're working with the terminally ill, to… And we're giving them the chance to live forever, just *differently*.

MEPHISTOPHELES. Of course I could pay them a visit – be persuasive.

FAUSTUS. No. We'll find some country somewhere to rubber-stamp it, but I can't keep wasting time. Ugh! I've been here too long. Got distracted. I think it was water on Mars, or HIV, or… no, stem cells – it's all still about the stem cells, actually, but I don't have the time to…

FAUSTUS *yawns.*

MEPHISTOPHELES. Still not sleeping?

FAUSTUS. I don't need to sleep. Paracetamol.

MEPHISTOPHELES (*handing over pills and water*). They don't do anything. You can't get sick.

FAUSTUS. I know.

MEPHISTOPHELES. The girl's here too.

FAUSTUS (*swallowing the pills*). The…? Oh right, yeah – bring her over.

MEPHISTOPHELES *nods to someone, and* JENNY, *a young recruit, is brought over. She's a little nervous.*

MEPHISTOPHELES. This is Jennifer Wagner. Jennifer, Doctor Faustus.

JENNY. Jenny, please. A pleasure – an honour.

FAUSTUS. You're the Franken-corn girl, aren't you?

JENNY. Yes.

FAUSTUS. Spliced regular corn with cacti DNA – same nutritional value but only requiring a third of the hydration. Smart – very smart.

JENNY. Thank you.

FAUSTUS. Tasted like shit. Made people sick.

JENNY. Yeah, we had some –

FAUSTUS. Someone died?

JENNY. No – no, not at all. We had one, uh, very bad reaction. Early on. Had to induce a coma, but…

FAUSTUS. No, but impressive. You were at Caltech but you didn't graduate.

JENNY. That's right.

FAUSTUS. You dropped out?

JENNY. Yes. Well no, I... My mum got sick.

FAUSTUS. You weren't studying medicine?

JENNY. No.

FAUSTUS. You couldn't help her.

JENNY. I –

FAUSTUS. You were halfway to feeding the world, but you threw all of that in.

JENNY. I didn't know how long we'd have.

FAUSTUS. Do you think that was selfish, Jenny?

JENNY. Selfish?

FAUSTUS. You do want to work here? You want to be part of the work we do?

JENNY. More than anything.

FAUSTUS. More than anything? Great. Glad to hear it. Except what happens when we're on the cusp of a breakthrough and your mother gets sick again and you leave us all in the shit to run away and play nursemaid?

JENNY *glances over to* MEPHISTOPHELES. *He offers nothing.*

Don't look at him, look at me. How do I know I can rely on you?

JENNY. I... Um... It isn't... She died. My mother died, so...

FAUSTUS. I see.

JENNY. I'm sorry. I'm not... I do really –

FAUSTUS. Oh, for the love of... (*To* MEPHISTOPHELES.) Give the girl a tissue.

JENNY. Thank you.

FAUSTUS. Listen, Jenny. It's not your fault your mother died, you understand that?

JENNY. Yes.

FAUSTUS. But she was always going to die. People die. Mothers die. My mother died a long, long time ago. And we're working on that, yeah? But until I solve it that is the reality of the situation. Where will we be in a hundred years, Jenny – in two hundred – what's your best guess?

JENNY. I don't know.

FAUSTUS. Guess.

JENNY. I'm not... Living on Mars? In nuclear bunkers? Wiped out entirely?

FAUSTUS. Okay. So. In two hundred years' time you and everyone you will ever meet will be dead, yes? Any survivor – if there are survivors – will be a total stranger to you. So why should we even bother? But I'm playing the long game. I'm trying to get my house in order. I've got to tend to the trees. Do you understand?

JENNY. Yes.

FAUSTUS. And I need people I can trust. I'm getting old – I won't be around forever.

JENNY. You're not old.

FAUSTUS. I'm older than I look. I need people who will do what it takes, who will think about tomorrow, not today, who have the capacity for greatness. Is that you? Should I let Jenny inherit my Earth?

JENNY. Yes. You can trust me, I promise.

FAUSTUS. Good. (*Offering her hand.*) Welcome to the Institute.

Scene ends. Into –

Scene Eleven

A boardroom. Waiting for FAUSTUS *are* WAR, FAMINE *and* PESTILENCE. *We see them more clearly now. They are as grotesque as we might hope, both human and not, rooted in an older time.* MEPHISTOPHELES *is with them.*

WAR (*to* MEPHISTOPHELES). You must answer for her.

MEPHISTOPHELES. I answer only to Lucifer. Let him come.

PESTILENCE. He sends us.

FAMINE. She has grown out of your control.

MEPHISTOPHELES. No.

WAR. Been allowed too much. Conceded too much ground.

PESTILENCE. She has placed a worm in his brain too.

MEPHISTOPHELES. She has her will, and Lucifer his ways.

FAMINE. I say you are enamoured by her.

MEPHISTOPHELES. Bound to her.

FAMINE. Grown too fond. Her lapdog. Poodle.

WAR. Cannot be trusted. The threat must be neutralised.

MEPHISTOPHELES (*snaps*). Her time is not yet up.

FAMINE. Yet every day she lives more lives are saved.

MEPHISTOPHELES. She must have every second she was given – every second that was promised her. Or would you make Lucifer a liar?

PESTILENCE. Every wretched second – right to the last. But we are coming for her, make no mistake.

The HORSEMEN *start to draw back.*

MEPHISTOPHELES. You are not needed! I shall see to it – she shall burn!

FAUSTUS *enters. She seems disorientated. She cannot see the* HORSEMEN.

FAUSTUS. Mephistopheles?

MEPHISTOPHELES. Here, Faustus.

FAUSTUS. I heard… I was sleeping, maybe. I heard talking, noise.

MEPHISTOPHELES. You slept?

FAUSTUS. I think a little. Was someone here?

MEPHISTOPHELES. Not a soul but us.

FAUSTUS. I was thinking – asteroids – have we talked about asteroids?

MEPHISTOPHELES. No.

FAUSTUS. Mineral-rich. Billons of tonnes. Just floating out there. No conflict in space. Just got to get to them. I've allocated the funding for a programme.

MEPHISTOPHELES. Excellent.

FAUSTUS. And Luxemburg – we're going to do the human trials in Luxemburg. All signed off.

MEPHISTOPHELES. Good news.

FAUSTUS. So we can move on. (*Beat.*) I'm so tired.

MEPHISTOPHELES. Don't worry, Faustus. You're on the home stretch now.

FAUSTUS. Good. Let's go. Ten years should do. Let's go.

A shift. A rumble. Rubble falls. WAR *comes forward.*

WAR. And in her absence
War has cracked a red raw fissure across the Earth
I have my fingers under its skin, inside its wounds
And I am squeezing, squeezing –

FAUSTUS. No –

WAR. Still, Faustus cannot surrender
Rolls up her sleeves and gets to work
Forges her science into weapons

    Bludgeons a weary world into submission
    Until we have peace again.

FAUSTUS. Mephistopheles! It's done. It's over. Twenty years.
Come on.

Another quake. More staggering, stumbling, destruction.
WAR *draws back and* FAMINE *comes forward to narrate.*

FAMINE. Now Famine takes her turn.
    Faustus finds the crops have failed,
    The new strains unsustainable
    Too perfect, too other, too alien to survive here.
    Good riddance.
    And if she had any sense
    She'd let me starve this bloated planet before it bursts
    But no.

FAUSTUS. I can fix this. Mephistopheles –

FAMINE. So tired. Dead tired. Bone tired.
    But she pushes on,
    Creates new techniques,
    Splices genes,
    Conjures water from barren rock
    Somehow
    Somehow she keeps going
    Until those who survive once more have bellies full.

FAUSTUS. Onward then! Fifty years.

More quake, as before. PESTILENCE *speaks.*

PESTILENCE. And here's the world in the grip of plague
    Here Pestilence reigns supreme
    Just as I did all those years ago –

FAUSTUS. I rid this once already – I can again.

PESTILENCE. I could dance this dance forever –
    Infection and inoculation,
    Thrust and parry,
    Sickness and cure.
    Oh, never in the nine circles of Hell

Was there such a torturer as her
For she simply will not give up
Even as her patients grow older and older
Sicker and sicker, sadder and sadder,
Until death holds no more fear for them
But is clawed towards with desperate longing.
She quarantines and disinfects,
Seals off whole cities,
Until finally –

FAUSTUS. Finally I am done.
Finally possess the knowledge
To extract minds from bodies and upload them
Humanity raptured up into the Cloud
Where war, disease and hunger have no place
No want, no pain, no hurt or suffering
No judgement. No damnation. None of it.
My silicon Utopia on Earth.
And I looked upon it
And saw that it was good.

She takes a breath. The HORSEMEN *come forward.*

What? Did you not think I could sense you? You don't play
fair, but I bested you all the same. So long War, farewell
Famine, Pestilence adieu. Where's the fourth then? Come on
– bring out the pale rider! (*Laughs.*) I thought as much.
Death is so scared of Faustus he won't face me. I've
banished him for good!

PESTILENCE *holds up a black robe, or produces a scythe,
or something along these lines.*

What's this?

PESTILENCE. Your destiny, as the fourth of our number. This
is the part you play.

FAUSTUS. No. Not true. I won. I saved them all.

*A final quiet rumble. The lights flicker and go out one by one.
The sound of generators gradually winding down until there is
silence.*

What is…? Mephistopheles? Light!

Lights start to creep back up dimly. Only FAUSTUS *and*
MEPHISTOPHELES *remain.*

What happened?

MEPHISTOPHELES. The power failed.

FAUSTUS. No, that's not… It can't. There are contingencies –
external, off-site… I was… Failed?

MEPHISTOPHELES. Yes, Faustus.

FAUSTUS. Everywhere?

MEPHISTOPHELES. Yes.

FAUSTUS. Lost?

MEPHISTOPHELES. Yes.

FAUSTUS. How much? (*Beat.*) Everything? (*Beat.*) Everyone?
All of…? I… I…

MEPHISTOPHELES. Yes.

FAUSTUS. Ten billion minds, housed in… Some of the back-ups
must have –

MEPHISTOPHELES. No.

FAUSTUS. No.

A silence.

MEPHISTOPHELES. So? You still have a little time.

FAUSTUS. I'm not… I can't… All of them?

MEPHISTOPHELES (*genuinely*). You have been spectacular,
Faustus. You have exceeded my every expectation.

FAUSTUS. I…

MEPHISTOPHELES. Chin up. All's done.

FAUSTUS. Yes.

MEPHISTOPHELES. What next?

FAUSTUS. Go.

MEPHISTOPHELES. The job's not finished. Think what we could now do – could now build.

FAUSTUS. This is the last command I shall ever give you. You are to take me one thousand years forward and there you shall leave me, never again to be in my sight, until the Devil comes to take his due.

MEPHISTOPHELES. Faustus –

FAUSTUS. And till that time – as much as might be left – you are to live by the code I could not. First do no harm. I bind you to that with all power I have.

MEPHISTOPHELES. Don't be rash.

FAUSTUS. That will be all. I cast you out.

The earth shudders. Into –

Scene Twelve

The far-flung future.

FAUSTUS *tends to a garden. She wears something simple/earthy – something not out of place on a seventeenth-century peasant woman. She speaks to us.*

FAUSTUS. The world is quiet now.
    And the world is healing,
    Finally given a chance to recover.
    I set about digging a garden
    And it blooms – oh, how it blooms!
    I tend to seedlings like they were my children,
    Ancient varieties and new strains,
    And the air is cool
    And the sun is pale and low

And I am not alone.
No, some survived –
Some stragglers who couldn't bear to have their mortal flesh
    uploaded –
And now, so many generations on,
Have no idea of everything they lost,
Or the role I played
But they come to me sometimes,
The woman in the woodland who seems older than her years
Who knows things she couldn't possibly know
And they ask 'How did you do that?'
And 'How do you grow that one?'
And I tell them how my mother taught me,
And how I'd gladly do the same for them.
They're grateful. For the most part they're grateful,
As I am grateful for them
In the moments I forget myself
And am just another woman in the woods.

ALICE, *a local woman, joins* FAUSTUS. *She holds a basket of mushrooms.*

ALICE. Found them just east of the creek – where the crooked firs grow.

FAUSTUS. Let's see. (*Looking through.*) These ones are good. These are safe to eat but the flavour is awful. Not these though – you see the white marks on the bottom? That's deadly.

ALICE. Got it.

FAUSTUS. But keep searching for more of these. They grow in clusters and they like the shade.

ALICE. Thank you.

FAUSTUS. I've just boiled some water, if you'll stay for tea?

ALICE I should get back before it's dark.

FAUSTUS. You'd be welcome to stay.

ALICE. I shouldn't. Thank you. (*Beat.*) They say... In the village they...

FAUSTUS. Yes?

ALICE. Doesn't matter. Only... A boy was passing, on his way
to the creek. He said he heard you talking to someone.

FAUSTUS. To myself, maybe. Comes from living alone.

ALICE. In a strange tongue.

FAUSTUS. I've travelled, yes.

ALICE. Frightened him.

FAUSTUS. Then he shouldn't have stopped to listen. (*Beat.*)
What can I say? I don't have much company.

ALICE. I'm sorry.

FAUSTUS. Don't be.

ALICE. Did you have someone once?

FAUSTUS. In a way.

ALICE. And was he with you long?

FAUSTUS. Oh, about a thousand years.

ALICE. The way you talk sometimes.

FAUSTUS. Promised me the world.

ALICE. They always do.

FAUSTUS. And to his credit he delivered a good part of it.

ALICE. But he wasn't kind?

FAUSTUS. That wasn't in his nature.

ALICE. No excuse.

FAUSTUS. Maybe. But he'll be back. Some day soon, I'd wager.

ALICE. I hope not. (*Beat.*) See those clouds scuttling over –
there's a storm in them.

FAUSTUS. Hmm?

ALICE. I saw earlier this big, black bird – biggest bird I ever
saw – always sign of a storm.

FAUSTUS. What kind of bird?

ALICE. Like none I've ever seen. Beat its wings and seemed to suck all the light out of the sky.

FAUSTUS. You should go. Sun's getting low. But come back and visit again soon.

ALICE. I will. I promise.

ALICE *smiles and goes. A pause.*

FAUSTUS. So it's time then.

FAUSTUS *sings softly to herself.*

(*Sings.*) 'Though some by age be full of grief and pain,
Till their appointed time they must remain;
I take no bribe, believe me, this is true.
Prepare yourself to go; I'm come for you.

Prepare yourself to go; I'm come for you.'

She stops. She speaks to an unseen presence.

Show yourself. Stop lurking.

LUCIFER *steps forward. Plague mask/beak, now perhaps with great black wings emerging from his back. She doesn't look at him.*

I've been expecting you. (*Beat.*) Hard to be precise – lost track of the days. So small, days. So then I moved to moons – twelve moons in a year – mark them off. Not exact, but... Then I thought about time zones, about chasing the light around the globe so the sun never set on me, and that way you could never claim my days were up. Loopholes. How does the Devil keep time anyway? Not with an atomic clock, not laboratory conditions, nothing so scientific. And I think – I think that's because it scares you – science scares you – because once we can explain something we have no need to fear it. I think you only have power in the dark. Lucifer. Light-bringer. Jealous of any other. I think you regret leading Eve to the apple – you thought you would be the one to teach her everything, but she blazed so much brighter than you ever dreamed of.

Anyway, I'm rambling. But I have been expecting you.
Knew it was soon. I took down the scarecrow, did you see?
That was for you. Big old crow. Big old bird. No use trying
to keep you out. So here we are then. Don't you have
anything to say?

LUCIFER *takes off his mask. He speaks as* THOMAS, *her
father.*

LUCIFER. Johanna –

FAUSTUS. Don't call me that. Call me Faustus. Call me Doctor.

LUCIFER. I have another doctor coming.

FAUSTUS. Too late for that.

LUCIFER. Be calm. What can you remember? I found you
collapsed on the heath – had to get you out of London – had
to bring you home.

FAUSTUS. Home?

LUCIFER. Look – this is the house you grew up in.

FAUSTUS. No. No, I built it to bear a resemblance, that is all.

LUCIFER. Please, child –

FAUSTUS. I am not your child. You are not my father. My
father's dead.

LUCIFER. Try not to –

FAUSTUS. He ran back towards the flames. How dare you
wear his face?

MEPHISTOPHELES *enters.*

LUCIFER. Ah, here is the doctor now.

FAUSTUS. There you are.

MEPHISTOPHELES. How fares the patient?

LUCIFER. Her mind is uneasy.

FAUSTUS. Stop playing – you know me – you *know* me –

MEPHISTOPHELES. I see. I fear she has her mother's madness.

FAUSTUS. No. I am not mad.

LUCIFER. She has been spinning the most incredible fantasies.

FAUSTUS. Do not call me mad. Call me wicked. Call me a
sinner. Call me wrathful, prideful, slothful, lustful, envious,
gluttonous, greedy, anything but mad. You may take my soul
but you cannot have my mind.

MEPHISTOPHELES. How long has she been like this?

LUCIFER. A few days.

FAUSTUS. Liars! You are liars. I haven't seen you for
thousands of years.

MEPHISTOPHELES. What year is it? Who is the king?

FAUSTUS. Please – I was cruel to you sometimes, but for all
we shared –

MEPHISTOPHELES. I do not know you, ma'am.

FAUSTUS (*faltering*). No –

LUCIFER. Hush now. You have been through so much – you
are so tired.

FAUSTUS. I am.

LUCIFER. You will sleep soon – sleep so soundly.

FAUSTUS. Father?

LUCIFER. Come here, girl.

> FAUSTUS *embraces* LUCIFER, *sobbing on his shoulder.*
> *He comforts her. Then* KATHERINE *appears behind him.*
> FAUSTUS *sees her.* KATHERINE *shakes her head.*
> FAUSTUS *recoils from* LUCIFER.

FAUSTUS (*quietly*). No. I know who you are.

LUCIFER. Johanna –

FAUSTUS. You never helped her.

LUCIFER. No –

FAUSTUS. At least I tried. God knows I tried. That might count for something.

LUCIFER. Calm yourself.

FAUSTUS. I am not mad, nor was my mother.

MEPHISTOPHELES. She's seeing things. She is quite delusional.

FAUSTUS. I know who I am. I am Doctor Johanna Faustus, MD, PhD, Nobel Laureate. I have eradicated plagues and cultivated bacteria on Mars. I have brought rain to the deserts and sucked poison out of festering wounds. I have cured the sick and healed the lame. I am the last in a long line of healers. I am the witch's daughter. I have magic enough of my own. And I am a multitude of things but I am not mad. You will acknowledge me.

MEPHISTOPHELES. So frail. She shall not last the night.

FAUSTUS. When the clock strikes twelve?

LUCIFER. Try to make some peace with the world before you leave it.

FAUSTUS. Who said I was leaving?

LUCIFER. You cannot fight this.

MEPHISTOPHELES. The mortal flesh is weak.

FAUSTUS. And your imagination is so small. So Faustus must die, as all must die, and Faustus must be damned, as Eve was damned, as all are of her sex. For she did not know her place. For she has overreached, and for that she must be punished. But leave the world? No, sirs, I'll none of that. For I have scattered seeds in the forest and I know not what they'll grow into. It's not my place to know – I see that now. I was never meant to walk amongst the trees I planted, but plant them in the hope that others would. Hope, sirs, not for my soul, but the ones who come after. And no, I shall not live to see them bloom. I shan't watch the buds unfurl and breathe in the scent of morning, and so I cannot say with scientific certainty that spring will come. But for the first time I have faith. Faith in my daughters. Faith in the ones that follow. And that is why Faustus may be damned, but she is not lost. That is why you fail. What? Do you have nothing else to say?

The clock strikes twelve. FAUSTUS *laughs as* LUCIFER *and* MEPHISTOPHELES *watch her. She seems in complete control. Then just before the final chime she suddenly looks up.*

Wait –

The last chime strikes. Snap to black.

End.

www.nickhernbooks.co.uk

facebook.com/nickhernbooks

twitter.com/nickhernbooks